Beer an

A celebration

Bill Taylor
Beer and Food
A celebration of flavours

with Alan Saunders

and Tony Bilson, Len Evans, Chuck Hahn, Robert Irving, Carol Selva Rajah *and* Richard Thomas

Recipes by

Barbara Beckett, Maggie Beer, Martin Boetz, Joan Campbell, Robert Castellani, George Diamond, Peter Doyle, Alain Fabrègues, Sue Fairlie-Cuninghame, Margaret Fulton, Louise Harper, Genevieve Harris, Janet Jeffs, Philip Johnson, Janni Kyritsis, Cheong Liew, Stefano Manfredi, Lyndey Milan, Gary Miller, Damien Pignolet, David Pugh, David Sampson, Kate Sparrow, Chris Taylor *and* Liam Tomlin

Photographs by Rodney Weidland, *food styled by* Peter Doyle

Beckett Maynard Publishing

Author's note

As a brewer I often have the opportunity to talk about beer but rarely to write about it. This book has given me the chance to really explore and expand on my favourite topics … for example, how beer is brewed, the difference between the many wonderful styles, how to pour a beer with a perfect foam and, of course how brilliantly beer partners food. I'm a brewer, not a writer, so producing a book is a little out of my comfort zone, but I have applied an important lesson I learned in brewing: I surrounded myself with talented people. When you read the names of those who contributed to this book you will understand why I am so fortunate. There are some, however, who are not specifically mentioned elsewhere. There are the great people at Castlemaine Perkins Brewery in Brisbane who introduced me to the theory and the joy of brewing. My family at home have been very supportive, especially my dear wife Annamaria who likes to test beer and food ideas in our kitchen. And I am especially thankful to have a managing director who is passionate about beer and to receive support from all the directors at Lion Nathan Australia. I hope you find something new and interesting here. Let's all learn how to better appreciate our beer.

BILL TAYLOR

PAGE TWO: *Philip Johnson's Salad of cuttlefish, pawpaw, chilli, lime and cashews, page 92.*

ABOVE: *Not everyone wants ice cold beer. Beer warmers are still used in Bavaria to gently warm the beer to a suitable temperature to best enjoy the flavour.*

RIGHT: *A perfect match. Fresh prawns with lime and balsamic accompanied by a white beer.*

Published by Beckett Maynard Publishing, a trading name of Barbara Beckett Publishing Pty Ltd and Debra Maynard and Associates Pty Ltd

14 Hargrave Street, Paddington, Sydney, NSW 2021, Australia

First published in 2002

© Copyright 2002 Beckett Maynard Publishing

© Copyright 2002 Chef and food writers' recipes are retained by those individuals

Edited by Debra Maynard and Phillip Rodwell; food editing by Barbara Beckett

Designed by Barbara Beckett; IT consultant Colin Seton

Printed in China by Everbest Printing Co Ltd

National Library of Australia Cataloguing-in-Publication data:

Taylor, Bill (Bill John), 1952-.

Beer and Food: a celebration of flavours.

Bibliography.

Includes index.

ISBN 1 875891 17 X.

1. Beer. 2. Cookery (Beer). I. Weidland, Rodney. II. Saunders, Alan, 1954-. III. Title.

641.23

All rights reserved. No part of this publication may be reproduced, stored in a retrieval system, or transmitted in any form or by any means, electronic, mechanical, photocopying, recording, or otherwise, without the prior written permission of the publisher.

Contents

Exploring beer, food too

1. **Welcoming beer back to the table** Alan Saunders 6
   How is beer made? Chuck Hahn 12

2. **What's in a beer? Bill Taylor 23**
   A glass act Bill Taylor 28
   A beer tasting Bill Taylor 34

3. **Styles of beer: ale, lager and their offspring Bill Taylor 36**
   Small breweries, big flavours Chuck Hahn 44

4. **The story of beer: from bread to breweries Bill Taylor 48**
   The Australian pub Robert Irving 60

5. **Matching beer with food Bill Taylor 63**
   Contemporary watering holes Alan Saunders 74

New flavours in the kitchen

6. **Light touches: snacks and starters 76**
   Foods that love beer Tony Bilson 84

7. **Hot days, cool flavours: summer mains 89**
   A wine lover's guide to beer Len Evans 100

8. **Cold days, warm comfort: winter mains 109**
   Beer and spice, a blessed partnership Carol Selva Rajah 118

9. **The icing on the cake: desserts 129**
   Cheese and beer marriages Richard Thomas 134

Biographies 139
Sources: text and historic illustrations 141
Index 142

Alan Saunders
1. Welcoming beer back to the table

Not fit for a prince

FERRIES dispatched from various points on Sydney Harbour began to land at Clontarf well before noon on the warm morning of 12 March 1868. Undaunted by the high cost of admission, large numbers of people made their way to the grassland above the cliffs, where those who arrived before midday could enjoy beer and oysters with brown bread and butter.

The object of the event—'A Grand Picnic,' as the organisers called it—was to raise money for a Sailors' Rest Home and to honour Prince Alfred, Duke of Edinburgh, first royal visitor to Australia. He, however, did not turn up until half past one, by which time the guests were tucking into chicken, lobster and champagne. In addition, many of them had, according to the *Sydney Morning Herald*, brought 'Copious supplies of even more ardent spirit.'

Some time after lunch, the spirits of the picnickers, already, one assumes, pretty ardent after all that grog, were roused to something like frenzy when one James O'Farrell, an Irishman of Fenian sympathies, took a shot at the Prince and wounded him. The royal victim was carried away unconscious and the crowd, denied the opportunity to lynch the man who had tried to kill him, fell instead upon the remainder of the food and drink. By the end of the day, 1,554 people had consumed 1,182 magnums of champagne and 798 bottles of beer: a substantial quantity of alcohol per head even without the other spirits they had bootlegged into the party.

It was, then, quite an Australian event: hot, crowded, noisy, not quite egalitarian, given the price of the tickets, somewhat ambivalent in its relationship to the ruling house of the mother country and, of course, boozy. The early and eager came for the beer and oysters; later, in deference to royalty, the food and drink obviously took a turn to the more genteel.

Beer and oysters—'unlimited supplies; consumption enormous', says the first Australian cookbook, considering the oyster in a survey of the aquatic resources of New South Wales in 1864—clearly won the popular vote. They were, and remain, a classic combination. At the Grand Picnic, the beer on offer was stout: a dark, toasty, hoppy brew whose happy marriage with the oyster was, according to the beer expert and historian Michael Jackson, the result of a chance encounter in the London of the early 19th century, where one was the drink and the other the food of the poor. Oysters from towns near the mouth of the Thames were plentifully available to the citizens of the capital until excessive dredging depleted their numbers.

This, perhaps, accounts for the status of the beer and oysters at Clontarf.

LEFT: *Stout and oysters are an enduring combination which came together when both were cheap and plentiful.*

Like much of the entertainment provided for the Prince on his tour, the Grand Picnic was a provincial event, not a colonial one. Australians wanted to show themselves off to this personage from the centre of Empire as sophisticated and worldly—drinkers of champagne, eaters of lobster—and doing that meant not drawing too much attention to a fondness for the meals of the London poor. In fact, they probably need not have been so wary: Benjamin Disraeli, still Prime Minister of Great Britain when the Prince first landed on Australian shores, had written of dining at that place of High Tory refreshment the Carlton Club on 'oysters, Guinness and broiled bones' after a Parliamentary debate. But that was in 1837, when the culinary culture of England was still one in which beer played an important part. It was a culture that, though it had left its mark on Australia, was in reality quite foreign. We have only to remember that in England at the time beer was drunk at every meal, even breakfast.

Quite an Australian event: an extremely well-catered picnic on the Hawkesbury River in NSW in the 1890s.

Beer with everything

When it comes to breakfast, the general rule seems to be this: you may be a way-cool global grazer who likes Portuguese salt cod for lunch, Thai green chicken curry for dinner and a nibble or two of baklava just before turning in, but you're likely to wake up to the same old Wheaties you had when you were a kid. This works both ways, of course—if you've been brought up to greet the dawn with pig's liver in rice porridge, you may not find poached kippers and Earl Grey very tempting—because breakfast is the most culturally defining of meals. It works historically too, so the breakfasts of the past, before tea, coffee, orange juice or muesli, seem to us more exotic now than whatever legendary groaning boards, laden with roast boar and a surfeit of lampreys, featured at dinner or suppertime.

So there is nothing better for bringing home to us a sense of the past as a foreign country—where even the licensing laws are different—than a quick look at what was on the menu when, say, Elizabeth I made her queenly way to the breakfast table. According to her household accounts for the year 1576, one morning she had cheat and manchet, ale and wine. In other words, she had bread and alcohol. Cheat is a form of bread made of coarsely-grained flour; manchet was made of more refined ingredients and consequently was more expensive.

The queen was not alone in waking up to bread and beer. At the beginning of the 16th century, the Earl of Northumberland and his wife could breakfast, even during Lent, on a loaf of bread cut into trenchers—so as to provide something solid off which they could eat—two small loaves, two pieces of salt fish, smoked herrings and fresh herrings or a dish of sprats, washed down, we are told by their household accounts, with a quart of beer and a quart of wine. At this time, measurements of capacity—such as pint, quart and gallon—differed somewhat from place to place and according to what was being measured, but it seems reasonable to assume that what these figures tell us is that the Earl and his Countess began the day with more than a litre each of wine and of beer. The children in the nursery were less extravagantly provisioned: they were allowed the beer but not the wine.

Both beer and bread (or, at least, leavened bread) are the products of fermentation and both owe their origins to the domestication of grain.

There is a certain consistency in bringing beer and bread together at breakfast. Beer, as the food writer Margaret Visser remarks, may be thought of as 'a sort of liquid bread'. Indeed, there is a long, ancestral connection between the two —both beer and bread (or, at least, leavened bread) are the products of fermentation and both owe their origins to the domestication of grain. In Medieval and Tudor England, even the law recognised that the one was almost as important as the other, because in order to protect the consumer, it regulated the production of beer almost as much as it regulated the production of bread.

'A sort of liquid bread': drinkers enjoy ale and flame-roasted meats in a sixteenth century English tavern.

Besides, in Northern Europe there had always been good reasons for drinking beer. You would not, on the whole, want to drink the water, drawn, as it often had to be from contaminated sources unless it had first been boiled, and brewing involves boiling. 'Water is not holesome sole by it selfe, for an Englysshe man,' wrote the physician Andrew Boorde in the first half of the 16th century, and the majority of his compatriots seem to have agreed with him, because all of them—kings, nobles and commoners—drank beer and drank huge quantities of it: at Ingatestone Hall in Essex in the middle of the 16th century, average daily consumption per head of small beer was a gallon, which means, give or take a bit, according to those differences in measures, around four-and-a-half litres.

The beer in question would have been brewed on the premises. Well into the 18th century, a cookbook like *The Compleat Housewife: or Accomplish'd Gentlewoman's Companion* would find it necessary to offer its readers a recipe for 'good household beer', and the down home nature of the English attitude to ale is made apparent in a book of the previous century, *The Closet of Sir Kenelm Digby*, where the recipe for ale with honey begins, 'Take forty Gallons of small Ale and five Gallons of Honey.' Still, however large the quantities in which it was produced, this home brew was, as the food historians JC Drummond and Anne Wilbraham remark, 'a good, sound healthful drink and one which could not possibly do any harm to children when drunk in reasonable amounts,' which might make one feel a little better about the Earl of Northumberland's kids.

The golden age of ale: an ornate silver tankard from the 17th century.

They took it not only as an everyday drink but as a celebratory drink as well. Medieval and Tudor England seem to have been the golden age of ale: that is to say, it was an essential part of feasts and other celebrations. There were Church Ales and Bride Ales; there were Whitsun Ales and Mary Ales; there was Cuckoo Ale, to celebrate the first cuckoo of spring; and Tithe Ale: a meal of bread, cheese and ale given by a priest to those of his parishioners who were liable to pay him a tithe (that is, a tenth of their income).

Beer was used for cooking too, of course. In medieval times ale was added to a green sauce of parsley and other herbs, together with garlic and pepper for serving with fish. Later the Elizabethans seethed shrimps in water and beer mixed together, while in the 18th century they were pickled in alegar. Alegar is to drinkable ale as vinegar—'vin aigre' or sour wine—is to drinkable wine, though nowadays it is better, if inaccurately, known as malt vinegar. Towards the middle of the century, Hannah Glasse's *The Art of Cookery Made Plain and Easy*, perhaps the most influential English cookery book of the 18th century, furnished a recipe for a rather surprising brown sauce for fish, using equal quantities of water and 'Small-beer, or Ale that is not bitter' together with mushrooms, an anchovy and some ketchup. In fact, the ketchup itself could have been made with beer: the chapter of Glasse's book addressed to the captains of ships encourages them to set sail with a powerful 'Ketchup to keep twenty years', which requires 'a Gallon of strong Stale Beer' as well as anchovies, shallots, mace, cloves, pepper, ginger and mushroom. 'You may carry it to the Indies,' Glasse says proudly, adding that 'the stronger and staler the Beer is, the Better the Ketchup will be.'

In Jane Austen's time, and in her world of provincial gentry, beer was still regularly drunk with meals, though the usual table beer was 'small' beer, with an alcoholic content as low as 2–3 per cent. But some of the most intriguing uses of beer in the 18th and 19th centuries were in what Maggie Lane, scholar of Jane Austen and her milieu, calls 'these hot, fortified, semi-alcoholic mixtures that fall somewhere between food and drink.' There was caudle, in which sugar, nutmeg and egg yolk were added to hot beer, there was apricot

Make a basic posset by boiling milk (or taking it straight from the cow), letting it cool and adding to it equal quantities of cider and beer with grated nutmeg, sugar and cream. For a sack posset, use sherry instead of cider (use half as much sherry as beer) with beaten egg yolks, bread crumbs and cinnamon.

Chuck Hahn

How is beer made?

Yeast organisms earn their keep by working around the clock in fermentation tanks, magically transforming the seasoned extract of malt into a flavoursome beer.

THERE are two answers to the question emblazoned at the top of the page. The first is that beer is made by cooking malted barley in water, boiling it with hops, cooling it, adding yeast and then letting the whole brew ferment and mature. Well that's the super-streamlined, in-a-nutshell version and it sounds fairly straightforward doesn't it?

The second answer is that good, flavoursome beer with a taste that lingers on the palate and eventually finds a little niche in the memory, is not just 'made', it is brewed and handcrafted with care and attention. Special malts are used, along with the correct hops to produce the spicy, floral, bitter finish, see *What's in a beer?*, page 23.

In practical terms, Australia's favourite beers come into being in the traditional way, in discrete batches which allows the brewmaster and his team to pay extra care and attention to the ingredients from the moment the malted barley goes into the mill to the clattering arrival of the first bottle past the labelling machine. So … to a day in the brewery—keeping in mind that unlike winemakers, brewers don't have a vintage. Beer is best drunk fresh so the labour of love at any brewery never stops!

Preparation Of course, as with any liquid that is intended to slide down the throat with ease, the main, but least exotic, ingredient is water. This is carbon-filtered to remove any impurities and the hardness or softness of the water may be altered by the addition of mineral salts. Elsewhere, malted barley is being crushed in a mill before being mixed with the water in a giant copper mash-tun.

Mashing The malt and hot water mixture is stirred vigorously in the appropriately named tun until it forms—you guessed it, a thick mash. The barley's fermentable sugars, crucial to the brew, are released during this process. This is not modern rocket science! As mentioned in *Matching beer with food*, page 63, beer began as a mealy gruel which some forgetful—or perhaps thoughtful from our point of view—person allowed to ferment. Of course that was so long ago that it's reasonable to assume that after a hard day building the Pyramids, the workers retired for an earthenware mug of mealy ale.

Lautering After a few hours, the two initial ingredients have been transformed into a porridgey mix and it's time to strain off, or filter (in German, lauter means 'to filter') the liquid, or wort. The grain husks go off to be recycled as cattle feed, and the clear malt extract flows on to the brew kettle. If the strange and archaic names are confusing, well … you can't deny brewers a few secrets, including the right to a traditional, private language that adds a little magic and mystery to their ancient craft.

Boiling This is where things really take off. Into a giant kettle goes the barley-based wort; it's brought quickly to the boil and is joined by the second important ingredient, the hops—the spice of the beer. The mix is boiled for at least an hour to extract the desired bitter flavours from the hops while still retaining their delicate herbal aromas. Further solids, called trub by the brewers—more esoterica for those who collect odd words—are settled out by a whirlpooling action and the 'hopped' wort is pumped away to be fermented.

Cooling and fermentation On its way to the tall fermentation vessels, the wort passes through a heat exchanger where it is cooled down to a fermentation temperature of 10–15°C. A special culture yeast is added (brewers call it 'yeast pitching') as the fermenter fills. The yeast converts, or metabolises, the malt sugars into alcohol, carbon dioxide and, of course, further beer flavours.

Maturation After a week of nature taking its bubbly, chemically reactive course, the result is beer … almost! The amber liquid is allowed to mature (this is called lagering from the German word 'to store') for two to three weeks at cold temperatures before being filtered. This last step restores clarity leaving a 'bright' beer that is ready for bottling or kegging and delivery to your favourite pub.

So that's how beer is made. Not that complicated but a job best left to the brewmaster and his dedicated crew. Throughout the process they must monitor the development of flavours by regular, careful tasting to assure that there is consistency in the brew (a tough job, but someone must do it). Give them a kindly thought next time you down a cool, sparkling lager—after all, for a modest price they have saved you an awful lot of trouble—unless of course you want to go back to basics and leave your winter porridge out in the sun to ferment!

Good, flavoursome beer with a taste that lingers on the palate and eventually finds a little niche in the memory, is not just 'made', it is brewed and handcrafted with care and attention.

ale and egg ale, and a variety of possets. Most of these were made with sherry, but there were a few that used ale, such as King William's Posset (ale, cream and eggs), or, from the 17th century, Kenelm Digby's 'Plain Ordinary Posset' (boiled milk with sherry, ale and sugar) and the very rich hot buttered posset that Elinor Fettisplace made from ale, sherry, curds, an egg ('shell & all'), sugar, butter and nutmeg.

'Lagerbier' for the colonies

'What two ideas are more inseparable than Beer and Britannia?' cried the Reverend Sydney Smith in 1823, '—what event more awfully important to an English colony, than the erection of its first brewery?' Smith, a noted writer and wit, was reviewing the report of JT Bigge, Commissioner of Inquiry into Lachlan Macquarie's governorship of New South Wales and he clearly agreed with the Commissioner that deficiency in the beer department was a very serious deficiency in a British colony. Macquarie had put up some fine public buildings—'A man who thinks of pillars and pilasters, when half the colony are wet through for want of any covering at all, cannot be a wise or prudent person,' Smith snorted—yet it took a great deal of effort to persuade him to build a brewery in Tasmania.

A healthy alternative to rum: in 1878, the Fitzgerald Brothers bought a rum distillery in Brisbane and created a successful brewery—still brewing on the same site.

This was more than a little hard on Macquarie, who, since his arrival in 1809, had done a lot to encourage the growth of brewing in the young colony, if only because he, like other early governors, thought beer a healthy alternative to rum. In fact, beer had been present from the very beginning of white Australia—the toasts drunk at Sydney Cove on 26 January 1788 were drunk in porter—and, according to the historian David Hughes, the brewing industry progressed rather more briskly than has often been supposed. Things were difficult at first, of course, because nobody knew how to farm this unfamiliar soil, but James Squire was brewing within a few years of opening his tavern in 1795. And, though the local barley was often of poor quality, Governor Macquarie thought highly of the hops produced in Sydney.

Tasmania, however, was more suitable to the production of hops, as Edward Abbott, a resident of Hobart, was happy to point out in his cookbook of 1864: 'The great heat in the Australias is prejudicial to brewing and malting, but Tasmania, being situate in a milder climate, has an advantage … '. Indeed, he looked forward to the day when ale from Tasmania would replace British bitter on the Indian market.

From the start, brewing in Australia was essentially commercial rather than domestic, but Abbott (who, though born in Sydney in 1801, was in many respects a transplanted Englishman) still thought it necessary to tell his readers how to brew their own strong beer. In some suggested menus for beer and food, he pairs 'strong beer' with rabbit curry, Indian chutney and rice, and, for 'Colonial family fare', porter with sea pie, boiled potatoes and vegetable marrow.' But he was very taken with Bavarian lager ('The "lagerbier" once introduced in the Australasian Colonies would, without doubt, supersede all other brewing …') and recommends serving it with New England chowder and cottage bread.

Abbott was not, though, really a beer man. Perhaps this prejudice in the mind of one of the colonial gentry reflects the falling status of beer in the mother country. In the England of Abbott's day, beer, once the table drink of the highest and lowest in the land, had given way in the best circles to tea or coffee at breakfast and wine at dinner. The respectable working classes and the Dickensian lower middles stuck with it, though: they could lunch at a tavern or eating house on meat, vegetables, bread, cheese and beer, then return home to similarly hearty fare with bottled beer. At around this time, Dr Phillip Kitchiner's *Family Oracle of Health*, setting out a plan of consumption for meals for 'moderate persons in a frugal family', allows one pint of beer per person a day, which seems very moderate indeed. But what did respectable Australians, in city or bush, drink with their meals? What they drank, in huge quantities and increasing numbers, was tea.

Some early breweries were suppplied by specialist maltsters: these men are spreading the barley in a 'floor' maltings to enable the grains to germinate. This moment in a working day was captured in 1920 at Joe White's Maltings, Melbourne.

The meal with no beer

Towards the end of the 19th century, the great music-hall performer Gus Elen was filling the theatres of England with his great, bellowing Cockney voice as he sang of his contempt for any drink that was not alcoholic:

> *Now for breakfast I never fink of 'aving tea,*
> *I likes a 'arf a pint of ale,*
> *For my dinner I likes a little bit o' meat,*
> *And a 'arf a pint of ale;*
> *For my tea I likes a little bit o' fish,*
> *And a 'arf a pint of ale,*
> *And for supper I likes a crust o' bread and cheese,*
> *And a pint and an 'arf of ale!*

In successive choruses, the novelist and social commentator Colin MacInnes tells us, 'the last line is varied to "a gallon and an 'arf" and then "a barrel and an 'arf"—bawled out defiantly, one may feel, at the Salvation Army lasses picketing the Music Hall doors outside.'

Regardless of whether a life of such alcoholic bliss was ever enjoyed by Elen's audiences, it seems that in Australia at around this time, beer at every meal was too remote a possibility even to be worth singing about. Shortly after World War I, Colin MacInnes, then a young boy, went to Australia with his parents. One of the products of their trip was *Trooper to the Southern Cross*, a sardonic little fiction in which MacInnes's mother, the English novelist Angela Thirkell, exposes the foibles and genteelisms of her husband's native land. So successful was she that many readers, even many Australian readers, thought that the book really was what it claimed to be: a memoir by one Leslie Parker, medical officer on board a troopship carrying diggers home after the war. Mutton, we learn from the book, was a big feature in Major Parker's childhood—understandably enough, since his people had a sheep station in the Western District of Victoria—but so was tea: for breakfast, there were mutton chops 'and plenty of tea'; for lunch (called 'dinner'), there was more mutton, and for dinner (called 'tea') there was shoulder of mutton, potatoes, tomato sauce, scones, fruit pies or jam tarts, cheese 'and plenty of good strong tea'. When Dad came home, he'd always greet Mum with one of two remarks: 'What about a cup of tea and some of Mother's pie?' or 'What about cooking us a chop, old girl, and a nice cup of tea?'

In the country, where sobriety was very necessary if the work was to be done, the bushman's weekly ration was meat, flour, sugar and tea. Henry Lawson sums up a bush Christmas of 1902 as, 'Mutton and plum pudding—and fifty miles from beer!'

By the time he has embarked on his medical career Major Parker feels free to choose between beer and tea at lunch (which now he calls 'lunch') and to indulge in a port and lemonade at dinner (which now he calls 'dinner'), but it is clear that for him beer is not a natural accompaniment to food. At some point the at-the-table drinking habits of the English seem to have changed as well for the same was apparently true in England well into the second half of the 20th century. The food historian Christopher Driver, summarising a survey carried out in Britain in 1955, remarks that most of those who took part drank tea with their meals, if they drank anything at all. But in Australia, tea had begun to dominate long before 1955. JT Bigge, whose report on New South Wales had been reviewed by Sydney Smith, was perhaps, as Robin Walker and Dave Roberts, historians of food and nutrition in New South Wales, point out, 'the first to remark on the constant drinking of tea by the colonists'.

He may have been the first, but he was the first of very many. 'It is amazing what a quantity of tea is drunk in the bush,' wrote another visitor, William Howitt, in the mid-1850s, adding that the equivalent of 1.7 litres was thought 'no extraordinary quantity for one person after the copious perspiration of a day's travel in this warm, dry country.' Thirty years later, Richard Twopenny, a journalist from South Australia, writing of life in Australian cities, remarked that tea was the national beverage, drunk with every meal, even by the urban middle classes. The colonists, he added, preferred not to drink beer with their food, but they drank it at every opportunity between meals.

In the country, where sobriety was very necessary if the work was to be done, the bushman's weekly ration was meat, flour, sugar and tea. Henry Lawson sums up a bush Christmas of 1902 as, 'Mutton and plum pudding— and fifty miles from beer!' Naturally, there were temperance movements in Australia, but when the Sydney physician Philip Muskett turned his attention to the failings of the Australian diet, it was an excess of tea, rather than an

In the heyday of the country pub—whether the grand Kurri Kurri Hotel or the diminutive Royal at Wombat—most drinking occurred unaccompanied by the pleasures of the table. Both photographs were taken in the 1970s by JM Freeland.

excess of beer, that troubled him. His celebrated book *The Art of Living in Australia*, published in 1898 and addressed to a nation of meat-eaters and tea-drinkers, exhorts his compatriots to adopt a diet more in keeping with their Mediterranean climate, to eat more salads and drink more wine, but beer does not seem to be a problem for him. Even the redoubtable Mrs Lance Rawson, offering household hints from a station in Queensland, seems to have thought that 'an extra glass of brandy, whisky or such like' at lunchtime was more of a problem than beer.

For many years pubs such as the ornate George Hotel in Ballarat—a product of the prosperous gold-rush days—served a free counter lunch.

Beer, then, was in an interesting position at the turn of the new century: neither a staple nor a problem but certainly too familiar to be thought cool. For the writer Hal Porter, growing up in Melbourne in the twenties, sophistication meant wine or ouzo and Metaxas brandy with restaurant meals, not beer. But for the average Australian worker, beer was the drink of choice ... and it was possible at this time to enjoy beer with a meal and, moreover, you might not even have to pay for the food: it was the era of the free counter lunch.

Working up a thirst

Travelling through Germany in the 16th century, the philosopher Michel de Montaigne observed that when the locals drank, they liked to stimulate their appetites with slices of bread sprinkled with salt and spices. This sort of thing happens all over the place and not just where beer is drunk. In 19th-century Spain, slices of ham or plates of almonds placed over glasses of sherry were known as tapas (from the word 'tapa', 'to cover'). They were there to keep the flies off, but also to make the customers thirsty and ready to drink more. In the United States, bar owners have over the years devised various means of stimulating the thirst which it was their business to quench: when caviar was a good deal cheaper and more plentiful than it is now, they offered that to their customers; in Reading, Pennsylvania, where beer was introduced by the Dutch, a plate of cold cuts and cheese served at a bar is known as a 'Dutch Platter'.

In Australia, as in England, a small charge was at first made for the bread and cheese that customers could eat with their beer, but competition between pubs soon caused some to drop the charge to encourage custom, and, naturally, once some had done it, all had to. The food on offer grew more extensive: 'On a table are laid out for all comers slices of beef, sausages, bread, cheese, and biscuits,' wrote Oscar Comettant, a French visitor to Australia in 1888. 'You pay 30 centimes for your glass of beer, and eat for nothing.' He remarks that there are some bars where it is possible to eat free without drinking anything at all. This might make one wonder whether something had been lost in the translation, though Richard Beckett, in his history of Australian food, quotes an elderly relative of his who describes the lavish counter lunches available in Adelaide at the beginning of the 20th century—boiled mutton, roast beef, pork, potatoes, pumpkin, greens—and adds, 'It was *expected* that you'd have a pint of beer with your meal.'

In fact, nobody except the customers seems to have liked the counter lunch. Restaurateurs disliked it because it drew customers into pubs rather than restaurants; the temperance movement disliked it because it saw a free lunch and a glass of ginger beer as the first step on the road to drunkenness; publicans hated it because of the vast expense. Clearly, though, only concerted action could put a stop to the custom. The licensed victuallers of Brisbane managed it in 1912, but an attempt to do the same thing in Sydney was foiled by a single dissenter until the Restaurant Proprietors' Association joined the fight and introduced strong-arm tactics: 'If we have any blacklegs we will ask the breweries to stop their beer,' said the Association's president, and that was that. In Melbourne, though, it took a world war and the introduction of six o'clock closing to put an end to the free counter lunch.

> 'On a table are laid out for all comers slices of beef, sausages, bread, cheese, and biscuits. You pay 30 centimes for your glass of beer, and eat for nothing.'
> OSCAR COMETTANT

Working up a thirst: Peter Doyle's Dukkah, page 81.

But it was not gone forever. By the 1920s and 1930s, the poet Kenneth Slessor was paying sixpence for a beer and enjoying a counter lunch ('sausages, pies, brawn, pigs trotters, pickled onions') in the pubs of Darlinghurst. According to Slessor, there were three hotels offering free counter lunches, though JM Freeland, historian of the Australian pub, reports that when the counter lunch returned in New South Wales, Victoria and Tasmania, it was no longer entirely free: 'for threepence, plus the price of a glass of beer, the famished could eat their fill of bread, cheese, boiled mutton, or German sausage'. They were famished because of the Depression and the free counter lunch had returned as a way of attracting customers when business was bad for the publicans. It saw out the economic hard times and the beginning of war but disappeared forever in 1941.

In the Barossa Valley it wasn't a barbecue; it was a 'chop picnic'.

The barbecue exemplifies the important role of beer in Australian eating. Everybody loves a barbie—the heady smell of burning meat, the often superfluous salad that refuses to be eaten standing up and the bracing coldness of beer straight from the can or the stubby.

Perhaps it's not surprising that the pub art of the period should have refrained from depicting the victims of the Depression tucking into a counter lunch, but, nevertheless, the distance between advertising and reality at this period is very striking. The pictures painted on glass with which Tooheys used to promote its beer in New South Wales pubs are among the most distinctive popular art of the period. For the most part, they depicted sport and other outdoor leisure pursuits, but a series of paintings commissioned from 1939 confronted the inner-city drinker with scenes of striking chic: men in tails and dinner jackets, white and black, beautiful women in backless frocks clustered around tables spread with white linen and drinking not, as one might expect, champagne but beer served in elegant glasses. Few of Tooheys customers would have drunk their beer in such smart surroundings but it was a diverting and highly successful fantasy.

You eat, you drink, you smile

'With dexterous jerk, I lift from out the ice-chest … two pots of porter. You eat, you drink, you smile.' This is Marcus Clarke, concluding his instruction for the proper cooking and serving of chops. That was in 1879 and it shows a clear understanding of what we see as the place of beer at the lunch table. Sixty years later, similar pleasures were being enjoyed by the descendants of German immigrants to the Barossa Valley in South Australia. The men would grill the meat and make billy tea, periodically (as Angela Heuzenroeder tells us in her book, *Barossa Food*) 'delving into their kitbags for another Schluck of wine or beer.' They didn't call it a barbecue, though: it was a 'chop picnic'.

More than the counter lunch or Edward Abbott's dinner of New England chowder and lager, the barbecue exemplifies the important role of beer in Australian eating. Everybody loves a barbie—the heady smell of burning meat, the often superfluous salad that refuses to be eaten standing up and the bracing coldness of beer straight from the can or the stubby—but perhaps we should have learnt to be a little more subtle when marrying food with beer.

We probably will not revive the beer breakfasts of Tudor England (though it's certainly worth considering) but we need to think seriously about serving beer with lunch and dinner and what place it might have in our cooking beyond its role in many batters and beef carbonnade. This book is both a demonstration of this thinking and a celebration of the marriage of food and beer.

Some of the more familiar culinary uses of food and beer are present here, but achieved with a new sophistication: there's beer batter courtesy of Joan Campbell and Maggie Beer, and, though a beer-enriched Irish stew isn't represented, there's Braised

What better way to celebrate the contemporary marriage of beer and food than with Tony Bilson's Steamed cured salmon with cabbage, page 116.

WELCOMING BEER BACK TO THE TABLE 21

Absolutely fit for a prince: Robert Castellani's Mother-in-law's cake made with porter.

oxtail casserole from Robert Castellani and Beef carbonnade from Janni Kyritsis. Margaret Fulton's Steak and kidney pie flavoured with beer and mushrooms strikes an agreeably traditional note too, as does Sue Fairlie-Cunninghame's interesting Fast beer soup, which, with its cinnamon and egg yolks, recalls the caudles of earlier times.

The combination of beer and Asian food is, as Carol Selva Rajah says in these pages, a blessed partnership, so perhaps we need not be too surprised by (though we're very grateful for) dishes like Lyndey Milan's Lamb with Thai mint dressing or Philip Johnson's Salad of cuttlefish, pawpaw, chilli, lime and cashews—'A perfect salad to match with a rich malty pilsener that has a hint of sweetness balanced by bitterness.' The combination of beer and Middle Eastern food, though, is decidedly intriguing: Garry Miller's Muhammara dip and Peter Doyle's Dukkah present a very pleasing alternative to beer nuts and chips.

What's most encouraging of all is the fact that every contributor to this book has given serious consideration to what beer is (or, rather, what beers are) and to the full range of flavours, sweet and bitter, that it offers. Hence the very specific nature of some of the ideas here: Stefano Manfredi's Crostini with peas, roast garlic and anchovies provides 'a nice foil for a malt-honey and hop-bitter pilsener'; Damien Pignolet's Lamb shoulder braised with parsley and ale matches the bitter beer with 'parsley, thyme and leeks, which provide herbaceous and earthy qualities with a slightly bitter finish'; and Genevieve Harris matches the dark-roasted flavour of stout with chocolate and nuts.

We've come a long way from that warm spring day in Clontarf more than a hundred and thirty years ago, but one likes to think that, the next time we serve beer during the visit of an important personage from overseas, we'll be as early and as eager as before but this time we'll save some of the beer and the oysters and brown bread and butter for the distinguished visitor.

Bill Taylor

2. What's in a beer?

WHAT'S in the typical drink of beer? Well, the basic recipe is fairly simple: water, malt—of one or more types, hops and yeast. But most importantly, there's the human element: there has to be a 'cook' to turn this recipe into an irresistible drink. That's where the skill and experience of the brewer comes into play—using the very best ingredients, in the right amounts and monitoring their progress when combined, to produce a flavourful beer.

Australian brewers seem to be exercising their skill, experience (and a little intuition) fairly well as Australians drink more than 90 litres of beer for every person each year. As much as we enjoy our beer we should never take it for granted—an occasional pause to look at it not just as a thirst-quencher but to consider the many beers available to us, their different flavours and aromas, is time well spent. Sometimes, we probably taste only a fraction of what we drink because we tend to quaff our lager. It's not difficult to miss the real flavour of beer if you indulge only in a cold tinnie or a bottle of lager, ice-cold. With drinking habits formed by a warm climate and often blokey, colonial traditions, it's easy to see how some of us have forgotten to appreciate that beer comes in more than one style and with the various styles comes a complex tapestry of flavours.

To increase your enjoyment of beer's flavour, try pouring a drink, a lager or ale, into a generously-sized wide-mouthed beer glass, even a wine glass.

ABOVE: *A broken hop cone reveals its prize—the yellow globules of resin, the seasoning prized by brewers for 900 years.*

Take a good sniff. The bouquet of beer is often subtle but it is an important part of overall flavour appreciation. Take a generous first taste and savour the 'sting' of the coldness combined with the bubbles—the carbonation. The bitter bite of the hops leaves its indelible mark as a satisfying aftertaste. Slowly top it up as you drink, and watch its colour and the swirl of the bubbles as they create more foam while you pour. As the beer slowly warms, occasionally swirl the glass and smell the beer again to enjoy the full flavour.

The problem with drinking directly from a bottle or a can is that you isolate your nose from the beer. You then have to rely on the vapours from beer splashing around your mouth to find their way into the back of your nasal cavity. If you take beer straight off the ice at zero degrees it is even more difficult to appreciate taste and aroma as very cold beer numbs the taste buds. All you get is the carbonic bite on the tongue, some muted malt sweetness and afterbitterness. It is refreshing and what many drinkers look forward to in a beer, but it is not flavourful.

I often pour an ale into a wine glass just to ensure I can swirl and sniff and coax out any shy aromas. I like to pour a generous foam because I think it is part of the unique presentation and enjoyment of beer. Foam has a wonderful texture; it concentrates the hoppy bitterness, enhancing the flavour.

To accompany food, beer that is just a few degrees warmer than it would be straight off the ice will offer more flavour without sacrificing refreshment. Many brewers make beers that refuse to fall simply into the category of ice-cold, hot-day refreshments. These are usually the ales and stronger beers that you might enjoy in winter rather than summer. In Adelaide, Southwark Old Stout at 7.4 per cent alcohol is a beer to sip and savour for the roasted, chocolate, even coffee flavours. Fremantle's Little Creatures brewery makes a full-bodied, intensely fragrant pale ale of 5 per cent alcohol and the Grand Ridge brewery in Gippsland brews an 8.5 per cent-strong Moonshine.

ABOVE: *Restrained beneath the crown seals of these bottles there's a wealth of big, bold flavours waiting to be released. The higher the alcohol content, the stronger the flavour.*

OPPOSITE, TOP: *Barley, au naturel on the stem, and three versions of the malted grain, pale and Munich for lager-style beer and roasted for stout.*

The world's oldest recipe

The essential ingredients of beer, described above, have changed little since early civilisation. As described in *How is beer made?*, page 12, the unique flavours of beer are created by turning raw barley into malt, mixing the malt with hot water to extract the fermentable sugars, boiling the malt juice (called wort) with hops, and fermenting with yeast.

Old-world traditions are upheld by Australian maltsters—this Munich malt reflects the style of malt made popular by German brewers in the 19th century and still in demand today.

Barley This is the ideal grain for brewing because once malted it is ready to release its fermentable sugars in the brewhouse mash; it also produces a clean-tasting beer. Barley has a husk (unlike wheat) that acts as a natural filter in the first stage of brewing. Even wheat beers take advantage of the benefits of barley, using a combination of wheat and barley in the brew.

Malt The person who gets the raw barley grains to the stage where the brewer wants to get his or her hands on them is called the maltster. The maltster prepares the barley by steeping it in water, allowing it to germinate, then drying it to produce malt. It is the final drying process that creates the different coloured malts used for making various styles of beer. Pale malt, used for lager, is produced by drying the malt at the lowest temperatures, whereas ale malts are dried at slightly higher temperatures, creating darker colours. Very dark malts, used for making dark beers such as stout and porter, are roasted in machines similar to coffee roasters.

Water Brewers call the water they use to brew beer 'liquor'. Different waters have different mineral contents and this creates subtle flavours in the final brew. For example, ales generally require harder water than pilseners. Many of Europe's famous brewing towns were distinguished by the desirable qualities of their water. Modern technology allows today's brewers to add or remove minerals to suit the style of beer they are brewing.

Hops The fruits or 'cones' of the hop vine give an appealing spicy, herbaceous or floral character to beer and, as described in *Beer, hops and … Hildegard*, page 51, have been the preferred 'herb' in brewing since medieval times. Hops balance the biscuity sweetness of the malt; they add aroma and create the unique herbal bitterness in beer. And there is no shortage of hop varieties at the brewer's disposal—from the delicately aromatic Saaz variety used in pilsener-style lagers to the more robust, bittering hops such as Australia's Pride of Ringwood, grown in Tasmania, or Britain's Goldings and Fuggles varieties.

Herbs and spices Brewers have used herbs to flavour beer for thousands of years. Long before hops became the beer makers' favourite aromatic ingredient (it also has superior preservative properties), herbs such as yarrow, myrtle, juniper, ginger and liquorice were used. Some modern brewers still use herbs and spices to create unique, specialty flavours. Coriander and orange peel are used to flavour Belgian wheat beer, and the Scots add heather to a local brew. An alcoholic beer containing ginger is made by Melbourne's Portland Hotel brewery.

Yeast Yeast is the magic ingredient in beer. Its ability to multiply and turn sweet malt extract into alcohol flavours and carbon dioxide wasn't understood by brewers until the pioneering work of Dutchman Anton van Leeuwenhoek and, later, Frenchman Louis Pasteur, whose 19th-century research is described in *Pasteur: the father of modern brewing*, page 52. There are two main styles of brewer's yeast—ale and lager. Ale yeasts work at warm temperatures and produce ales, wheat beers, some specialty styles like Germany's altbier, and stouts. Lager yeasts are suited to the lower temperatures used to brew lager. Fermentation is slower, producing less fruitiness and more carbonation. Note that traditional English cask ale is often 'flat' and lager has a 'gassy' bite. The flavours in beer vary according to the ingredients—the type of malted barley, hops, yeast and any additional herbs. It's the yeast that transforms these ingredients and imparts its own unique thumbprint of flavours.

ABOVE: Hops are harvested, vine and all. The cones from these five-metre-long vines will be picked mechanically under cover.

LEFT: Ripe hop cones in a Tasmanian field await the harvester.

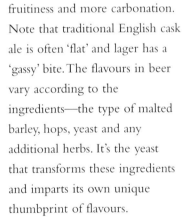

And what else does beer contain? There is alcohol, vitamins (particularly the B-group), minerals such as calcium, magnesium and phosphorous, and a small amount of protein and carbohydrate but no fat. Brewer's yeast contains essential trace minerals, such as selenium, chromium and copper in amounts comparable to fresh fruit and vegetables.

Bill Taylor
A glass act

Pay the world's brewers the ultimate compliment by matching an appropriate glass to the beer and pouring—not tipping—your beer to form a fine head that flatters the drink.

WHAT is the best container in which to serve beer? Well, if you want to experience the full range of taste, aroma and appearance of a fine beer then a good, well-shaped glass is far and away the best choice—certainly no other container so perfectly enhances the look of the beer and displays its foamy collar to best effect. Choose a glass that feels good and is not too heavy. Restrict drinking straight from a 'stubby' bottle or a beer can for the beach and the bush.

Tall slim glasses with a narrow base and a wide mouth are ideal for lager. They enhance the colour and clarity of the beer as well as helping it form and maintain a good foamy head as it is drunk. Elegant, stemmed glasses and flutes are also well suited to lagers, especially at the table. When dining, it is best not to fill the glass to the top—fill it about three-quarters full and ensure a good head. As you drink, top up your glass with cold beer to revive the foam and maintain a good presentation. Holding goblets and flutes by the stem is ideal because it prevents the hand from warming the beer.

... a well-poured foam has architectural integrity, like the trusses in a roof.

Goblets and samplers are best for ale because they allow the aromas to be more fully appreciated. Ale is also at home in a wine glass. The traditional straight glass and dimple mugs are fine in the pub but certainly not as elegant or as effective for appreciating the drink's aromas.

So forget about your dusty old stein and grandad's pewter mug. Keep the tumblers in the kitchen cabinet for fruit juice. Buy some good beer glasses or use your best wine glasses and flutes and, hey presto, you will truly engage your senses in the pleasures of fine beer drinking.

Drinking vessels, various

Beer drinkers in ancient Egypt refreshed themselves from individual clay pots. By the Middle Ages, drinking vessels were made from wood, porcelain, silver, pewter, glass and even leather; there was no distinction between wine and beer glasses until the 17th century. Glass was expensive because each glass had to be individually blown. By then the standard English ale glass was a stemmed flute similar to the flutes of Champagne although many patrons preferred to drink from their own mugs in the taverns and inns of the day.

In the late 18th century, the preparation of food, table settings and table manners—in other words the culinary codes that would continue until the present day—were taking shape. This was the innovative period of the industrial revolution which paved the way for large-scale glass manufacture. Lager brewing evolved, followed by refrigeration, boosting lager as a beer style. Glassware from Bohemia became highly regarded at around the same time the first golden pilsener beer was launched. The colour and clarity of lager and pilsener could be enjoyed in this fine, clear glass. Before long glass became affordable for everyday use.

Pouring: more than meets the eye

This may come as a shock, but contrary to popular opinion, beer is best poured directly into a glass that is *not* tilted. Slowly fill about a half to three quarters of the glass, adjusting the way the head foams by moving the pour on the side of the container if necessary. The idea is to create a generous foam easily. Stop and let the foam rest. It will consolidate and form a dense layer. After 20 or 30 seconds, finish pouring. The foam should rest just above the rim. A truly inviting sight. The foam will also leave tide washes down the glass as you drink. It will be

Few things are more fun to practise than the art of the perfect pour: don't tilt the glass, create foam at the bottom, fill it to the level shown in the middle photograph, wait while the foam rests, then finish pouring.

more resistant to the fats in food, which tend to collapse foam. I am fond of saying that a well-poured foam has architectural integrity, like the trusses in a roof. When you pour the beer as described above you'll know exactly what I mean.

A clean glass is a good glass

Beer glasses need to be treated with even more respect than your best wine glasses. If a glass is dirty the head won't rise as it is meant to. Disaster! It is best to wash glasses in detergent with a bristle brush to get rid of any grease. The secret is to thoroughly rinse them afterwards in cold water to get rid of any lingering detergent. Air drying avoids the risk of fibres from a tea towel sticking to the glass. Hold the glass up to the light to ensure it is thoroughly clean. It is worth the effort, as you'll discover when you pour a beer with a perfect foamy head.

Sniff before you taste

The best way to become acquainted with the bouquet of beer is to swirl your glass and take two or three short sniffs. Like wine, beer has a bouquet that varies from one style to another. Keep in mind that your sense of smell is surprisingly powerful—about 50 times more sensitive than your capacity to taste, and it is mostly underused when it comes to beer. Aroma magnifies the flavour experience when the beer is tasted because aromas are taken in through the back of the mouth as well as the nose when eating or drinking. These aromas stimulate sensitive receptor cells that send messages direct to the brain.

Variety is the spice of beers for they are certainly not all the same—a wide variety of aromas and tastes awaits the curious drinker. To fully appreciate the aromas drink from a glass rather than a bottle or a can.

There are lots of aromatic nuances to discover in beer. There are often fruity aromas in ales, and some are more citrus or floral or banana-like than others. Stouts and porters often have coffee or chocolate aromas. For example, James Squire Porter from

Sydney's Malt Shovel Brewery has a rich chocolate bouquet. German Erdinger wheat beer has a clove-like aroma.

Lagers can have grassy or pine-type, spicy aromas from hops. The aromas can be suggestive of fresh bread, biscuits or reminiscent of cooked corn from the malt, or fruity from yeast. Singha beer from Thailand has some fruity aromas from yeast, Steinlager from New Zealand has pine aromas and a hop spiciness, and Beck's from Germany has a cooked-corn character from malt.

Generally, we are much better at describing tastes than aromas. We seldom describe aromas accurately and use generalisations such as 'this smells wonderful' if we like something. Try taking a good sniff of the beer you're drinking and experiment with identifying and then trying to accurately describe the aroma.

... your sense of smell is surprisingly powerful—about 50 times more sensitive than your capacity to taste.

Let your taste buds run free

Discovering a particular flavour is what happens when the aroma combines with the taste. We taste sweetness at the tip of our tongue, bitterness at the back, sourness at the sides and saltiness is spread around but is mainly at the front (saltiness and sourness are not typical tastes found in beer). The caramel sweetness of an ale hits the front of the tongue. The bitterness of a pilsener blooms on the very back of the tongue.

Human beings can detect low levels of sweetness, around one part in two hundred, saltiness about one part in four hundred. We are most sensitive to bitterness and can detect about one part in two million. The taste buds at the back of the tongue are coarse and the bitter components—in the case of beer, from the hops—have to dig deep to be perceived. This takes a little time but the sensation lingers and brewers call this residual taste afterbitterness.

The ability of the staff to pour a fresh tap beer with a proper, tempting head can make or break a pub's reputation.

Consistency: the brewer's pursuit

One of the most unexplored things about beer in Australia, given most drinkers' preoccupation with thirst-quenching lager, is the diversity of flavour—from pale ale to stout, from pilsener to bock. However, unlike wine, a particular brand of beer rarely varies in its consistency of taste. Consumers demand that brewers pursue quality and consistency from the barley fields and hop gardens, and at every step of the brewing process. It is interesting that a drinker of beer demands such a high level of consistent flavour when

No matter which beer you choose—mainstream or boutique brewery—store it properly and drink it within two weeks.

the same person will happily accept a winemaker's advice that this year's vintage is a little different. As a brewer, I couldn't tell a beer drinker that a new batch of a particular style of beer is a little less bitter, more astringent or a little flat.

A drink to be drunk, not stored

Beer flavour is adversely affected by age, high temperature and light. Beer over the bar and out of the tap always tastes so good because it is better protected in cool storage and it never sees daylight in a keg. When buying beer remember that, like fruit and vegetables, fresh is best. Beer usually has a 9–12 month shelf life if conditions are good. If it goes stale, its flavours become papery or cardboard-like. In extreme cases, sherry-like flavours may even occur. It is unlikely that you would get old beer from a drive-in bottle shop or when buying a mainstream brand because of high turnover. The risk of finding stale beer is more likely with some imported or boutique beers that may be slower to move off the shelves. Some brewers use packed-on dates on their beers while others use 'best-before' dates, so always have a look at the date codes on cartons or bottles. Look for the best and buy fresh; I try to drink beer that is less than three months old.

It is best not to buy more beer than you need for the two weeks after purchase. Warm temperatures accelerate the ageing process: for every 10°C increase in temperature the rate of ageing doubles. That means beer stored at 20°C will age at half the rate of beer kept at 30°C. It is wise not to store beer in a place where it's going to heat up, such as a corrugated-iron garden shed. It keeps better in a cool, well-ventilated place. Beer also becomes stressed if the temperature varies repeatedly from hot to cold. For example, this happens in the boot of a car when it is hot during the day and cold at night. Treat beer as you would food items that you want to keep fresh and you will be rewarded with fine-tasting drink.

Light is also the enemy of good-tasting beer. It is always best to buy beer in a sealed carton. If you are buying beer off the shelf in a six-pack or by the bottle, take it from the shelf furthest from the light. Half an hour in direct sunlight or a few days in fluorescent light can give beer a sulphury smell that brewers call light-struck. The reason for this is that light affects the bitter hop flavours, setting off a reaction that produces the sulphur-like aroma. Even beer bottles sitting under fluorescent light in pubs' beer fridges can become light-struck. The good old brown beer bottle protects beer from light while green glass is not very effective as a light filter—but it looks good. Clear glass beers generally use a special imported hop that is unaffected by light.

Dark and cool is best

When storing beer at home keep it away from the light. Leave it in the carton and make sure it is kept cool. Store it in the fridge or in a well-ventilated place under the house. Chill the beer at least 24 hours ahead of drinking to ensure the carbon dioxide has a chance to stabilise in the low temperature. If beer is snap-chilled it doesn't pour well and can froth over when opened. If unintentionally frozen, then thawed, the flavour of beer is irrevocably damaged. If you chill beer on ice in an insulated container make sure it is not exposed to sunlight; keep it in the shade or keep the lid closed.

Above all, get your money's worth and don't forget to truly enjoy your beer. Use your best glassware, pour the beer to create foam at the bottom of the glass for a lasting head, and sip and savour as described in *A glass act*, page 28. Try some of the wonderful recipes in this book, and choose a beer, using *Beer and food matches*, page 72, to complement or contrast with the flavours of the food. We now have more beer styles to sample than there has been for more than a century. In fact, there has never been a better time to explore and feast on the flavours of beer.

We now have more beer styles to sample than there has been for more than a century. In fact, there has never been a better time to explore and feast on the flavours of beer.

Bill Taylor
A beer tasting

A beer tasting—how to gain new insights into the world's oldest alcoholic drink while enjoying a convivial social occasion. The ideal finger food to serve is a hard cheese like cheddar and crudité.

BEER drinkers, more so than wine drinkers, are often fiercely loyal to 'their' particular style or brand. That's why tastings can be fun: they often shed some suprising new light on beer loyalties. I have seen many drinkers change opinions on their favourite tipple when that familiar label is not there to guide their choice!

A beer tasting offers all sorts of possibilities but the main aim of the organiser should be to keep it simple and make it fun. Professional beer tasters use tasting sheets and concentrate on a silent assessment—not much fun for a novice group! Ensure some relaxed discussion about each person's assessment of the beers. While a sociable atmosphere makes it easier for everyone to make a contribution, the session is best steered by a leader to keep it on course.

To begin, a decision on the selection of the beers to be tasted is required. It might be a selection of lagers from around Australia or the world, or it might involve a mix of styles. It is wise to start with the lighter tasting beers in the selection and move through to the stronger beers. Buy fresh beers to properly appreciate the true and typical flavours. I never have more than ten beers for a tasting; for a social event six would be sufficient. Tasting can be done with as little as 50 ml of beer, so one stubby is enough for up to seven people. A very important part of a tasting is keeping a good supply of post-evaluation beers on hand to stimulate a spirited discussion!

Have a selection of small glasses so that everyone uses the same shape of glass and has one glass for each beer. This can present some logistical problems so an alternative is to have jugs of water on hand for palate cleansing and glass rinsing. Tasters can then reuse the same glass. Ice buckets can be used for rinsings. Don't forget that judges swallow their beer to get a full appreciation of the aftertaste so there has to be a rule that nothing other than rinsings goes into the buckets!

I always recommend that the organiser introduce the beers and provide some information about them including advice on how best to taste them. It is a distraction to have people guessing at what to do, or worse, copying the tasting methods of others. Having described the types of beer it may help to give the participants the relevant alcohol contents and any other information, but for extra fun keep the brand names secret until the end of the tasting. Allow the tasters to sample at their own pace and they may be motivated to make a few notes along the way.

Chill the beers to the appropriate temperature. A fridge temperature of about 4°C is good for lagers and a few degrees warmer is good for ales. Do not chill the beers on ice because the palate numbing cold will tend to deaden the taste of the beer. To ensure a vigorous discussion all tasters should share the one table.

To encourage a relaxed, sociable atmosphere it may help to have some tasty 'finger food' available to taste with the beers. Tasters can sip and savour the beer and then retaste after having had a snack. This is where sharing impressions of the beers with fellow tasters adds to the fun and learning. Remember that someone next to you may have picked out that elusive flavour you couldn't find a name for. Tasting is by its nature a personal thing so no opinion is right or wrong but merely another perspective. Here are some tips on what to look for:

Appearance Hold the beer up to the light. Look at colour and clarity. A dark beer may have a red hue. If there is cloudiness is it a heavy yeast haze or a fine protein haze? How would you describe the foam?

Aroma Swirl the glass and take two or three short sniffs to capture the aromas. Beers that are too cold may suffer an aroma loss. Is it fruity or spicy, floral or roasted?

Taste Sip the beer and let it wash over the tongue before swallowing. Is it sweet and malty or dry and bitter? Also consider the body. Is it a full-bodied or a thin beer? Is it creamy and smooth or has it an effervescent bite?

Aftertaste Does the beer have a lingering bitterness or maltiness? Aftertaste may be pleasantly bitter, roasted or astringent.

Balance Consider the overall interaction of tastes, body and aromas. It may be a drinkable, refreshing style of beer, or a sipping, savouring type. Would you want to taste this beer again?

Three beer tastings worth following

The beers are listed in a suitable order for tasting. Cheers!

Aussie lager tasting

NSW	Hahn Premium Light
TAS	Cascade Premium Light
QLD	XXXX Gold
NSW	Tooheys Extra Dry
VIC	Victoria Bitter
QLD	XXXX Bitter
TAS	James Boag's Premium
WA	Emu Bitter
SA	Southwark Bitter

A mixed style tasting

Lager	Tooheys New
	Hahn Premium
Ale	James Squire Amber Ale
	Coopers Sparkling Ale
Pilsener	Matilda Bay Pilsner
	James Squire Original Pilsener
Wheat Beer	Redback Original
	Hahn Witbier
Stout	Southwark Old Stout
	Coopers Best Extra Stout

International tasting

Mexico	Corona
USA	Budweiser
Belgium	Stella Artois
New Zealand	Steinlager
Germany	Beck's
Czech Republic	Pilsner Urquell
Thailand	Singha
England	Boddingtons
Australia	James Squire Amber Ale
Ireland	Murphy's stout

Bill Taylor

3. Styles of beer: ale, lager and their offspring

THERE are many styles and thousands of brands of beer made around the world—as many and varied as there are nations and national characters. All these beers are characterised by regional influences and brewing traditions as well as the different kinds of ingredients available, be it barley malt, wheat, specialty malts or hops. The styles I describe in these pages—from pale ale to stout, lager to bock, and wheat beer to vintage styles—all generally fit into the two broad categories of ale or lager. Understanding the difference between the two and being able to recognise each type by colour, aroma and taste, is akin to appreciating the differences between red wine and white wine or whisky and brandy.

There are major differences between ales and lagers: ales are more complex and robust in aroma and taste and are often darker in colour. There are many kinds of ale—from pale and amber to dark and strong—and the category also includes wheat beer, stout and porter. By contrast, lagers, the style of beer most commonly drunk in Australia, have more subdued flavours because of cold maturation. There is often an emphasis on bitterness, but lagers have a less intense aroma than ales and are usually paler in colour. Lagers are generally thirst-quenchers. They include the light, mid-strength, full-strength and premium lager brands popular in Australia and New Zealand. One of the best known lager styles is pilsener—first brewed in Bohemia in the mid-1800s, and now the most imitated style of lager in the world.

In Australia, with our temperate climate, it's the golden lager styles that are favoured. Some are moderately hopped and refreshing like Tooheys New or Carlton Draught. There are mid-strength lagers like XXXX Gold or Carlton Midstrength Bitter that offer a fine balance between malt flavours and hop bitterness. You might choose a premium lager such as Hahn Premium, which is brewed with a blend of special hops, for a distinctive flavour. Also popular, particularly in summer, are the dry-finish lagers, which are fermented for longer, like Tooheys Extra Dry.

But look beyond lagers and there are many good ales to be had. Take a look around the pub or bar next time you visit and try to spot an ale. It could be a fine Aussie ale such as James Squire's Amber or Coopers, or a traditional English ale such as Boddingtons or Tetley's. In Australia's temperate climate we tend to look for thirst-quenching varieties. But on a cold evening, take a tip from the Belgians and try an 8.5 per cent strong pale ale called Duvel as an aperitif, or a glass of Belgium's 9 per cent Chimay Blue ale at the end of a meal.

LEFT: *The colour of beer comes from the malt and the experienced brewer's palette of malts can produce many subtle colours and flavours.*

There are many styles and thousands of brands of beer made around the world—as many and varied as there are nations and national characters.

Vintage labels are evidence that ales, lagers and stouts have long been popular.

One of my fondest memories of ale concerns a vintage ale I had the joy of releasing to celebrate the arrival of the new millenium. It was brewed with a blend of specialty malts and had a delightful reddish hue to its dark colour. This Hahn Special Vintage was about 8 per cent alcohol, fermented with a Belgian ale yeast in the brewery and then with a second easily sedimenting yeast in the bottle. After two months of bottle conditioning in a temperature-controlled warehouse, the beer was released. It was strong, bitter, fruity and complex and I enjoyed drinking it from large goblets, wine glasses or brandy balloons at 8–10°C. As a nightcap it was wonderful. I enjoyed it with hearty casseroles in winter and with Christmas cake in summer. I still enjoy it as it ages gracefully. The fruitiness has mellowed to more dried fruit; the spiciness has merged with the maltiness and the beer has fermented a little further and is quite dry. And this ale still has further potential for ageing with yeast influences yet to fully take hold.

Ale or lager?—it's all in the fermentation

It's the yeast that makes the difference between ale and lager—the type of yeast and the temperature at which the beer is fermented and matured. For ale, the fermentation process takes place at a relatively warm, ambient temperature, and takes only a few days. Ale yeast is a top-fermentation yeast, so-called because it floats to the top of the fermentation tank. This warm process and this top-fermentation type of yeast give ale a unique aroma that I often describe as fruity.

I was introduced to English ales more than 25 years ago. It was one of the hottest summers to occur in England for hundreds of years and it gave me a great insight into why ales lost favour to lagers in Australia. The English pubs were overflowing with drinkers looking for a refreshing beer. It was a defining time in British beer drinking history. That summer propelled the sales of lager to new heights and broke down prejudices against the cold, carbonated drink. Ale never regained its dominance.

Ale brewing is an ancient process and the open tanks and room temperatures make life easier for the brewer. This is why they are a suitable choice for small brewers and pub breweries. Home brewers usually start their brewing experience with ales. Being brewed at warmer temperatures than lager, ales are sometimes served relatively warm, particularly in the UK and Europe. A temperature of 5–10°C brings out the flavour of an ale, and the higher alcohol ales can be served even warmer.

In contrast to ales, lagers are brewed with bottom-fermenting yeasts at much cooler temperatures than for ale. The lower temperature slows down the fermentation and the yeast sinks to the bottom of the tank. It takes a week or more to ferment and is followed by a cold-storage period of one week to as many as 12 weeks, depending on the brewer and style of lager.

Ale—an affectionate profile of the oldest beer

What I especially like about ales is the diversity of their colours and tastes. Some are pale while others are deep golden, amber, auburn or almost black. Some are cloudy from bottle or cask conditioning, where the beer is unfiltered leaving yeast in the bottle or cask. The alcohol content of ales is generally higher than lagers—a legacy of ancient brewing techniques. The higher alcohol level helps to prevent bacteria spoiling the beer. The English brewed a style called India pale ale—stronger in alcohol and with more hop bitterness than local ales—to help the beer survive the sea voyage to India. Coopers Sparkling Ale has a 5.8 per cent alcohol content and imports such as Belgium's Trappist Chimay beer go to 9 per cent.

The characteristic aromas of ale are fruity from the yeast, toasty and roasted from malt or spicy from hops. A good example of ale's toasty characters is Tooheys Old or James Squire Porter, both of which are great drinks with char-grilled steak. For spicy hoppiness, try Little Creatures Pale Ale; it's excellent with curries as a foil to the spice and a taste bud refresher. A great example of fruitiness can be sampled in the Belgian Duvel, which means devil in English. The pale golden but cloudy appearance does not hint at its 8.5 per cent alcohol content. I always drink it from a wine glass to swirl the beer and appreciate the luscious, fruity aroma. It smells, as strange as it may sound, like a glass of alcohol-infused fruit salad. Delicious. Some of the same flavour compounds that occur in apples, pears, bananas and other fruits are produced by ale yeast, and the warm ale process magnifies them.

If you're on the lookout for ales, I recommend the boutique brewers for variety. Visit the Lord Nelson Brewery Hotel in Sydney and try Victory Bitter or Old Admiral with steak and kidney pie. The Malt Shovel Brewery's James Squire Amber Ale has a rich roasted malt character and it goes well with roast beef. I like the rich, smooth character of the real ale, Smith's Special Bitter, at the Wig & Pen Pub Brewery in Canberra. Or if you're in Tasmania try a Hazards Ale on tap.

Pale ale This style is characterised by golden to copper colour, medium bitterness and fruitiness. Brewers use lightly kilned malt to produce the pale colour. In Australia, Coopers and Southwark of Adelaide, Cascade of Hobart, Little Creatures of

Fremantle, the Portland Hotel Brewery in Melbourne and Sydney's Lord Nelson brew pale ales, and the Malt Shovel Brewery in Sydney makes the variant India Pale Ale under the James Squire brand.

Amber ale As the name suggests, these ales are amber to copper in colour, have a rich maltiness, some fruitiness and a pronounced bitterness. Boutique breweries have lifted the profile of amber ales. I recommend trying James Squire Amber Ale or Grolsch Amber Ale imported from the Netherlands.

Brown ale These ales are copper to brown in colour; they have a medium malt sweetness and some fruitiness. They are different from amber ales because of more subtle malt and hop characters. Kent Old Brown is brewed in Sydney for the local market and some small brewers, such as the Sunshine Coast Brewery, which makes Robinson's Brown Ale, occasionally offer this style, but it is not widely available. Britain's biggest selling bottled ale, Newcastle Brown Ale, is available in Australia and some bottle shops stock Belgium's De Koninck.

Dark ale Dark ales have a deep copper to black colour. They are medium bodied, with medium bitterness and have some caramel notes and fruitiness. A few of these 'old' style ales have survived the prominence of lager. Try Tooheys Old, Newcastle Old, Coopers Dark Ale or Robinson's Dark Ale.

Red ale Red ales hail originally from Ireland and range from red-amber to red-brown in colour. They have a medium hop bitterness but often little hop aroma. They have a caramel, malty sweetness and a medium body with low levels of fruity fermentation aromas. Generally red ales are not brewed in Australia but occasionally a small brewer may have a red ale on offer. Ned Kelly's Irish Red Ale is brewed by Cheers Brewery in Brisbane, and the Wig & Pen makes Ballyragget Irish Red Ale. It's possible to sample imported Caffrey's, Kilkenny or Beamish Red ales on tap in Irish theme pubs, or try specialty bottle shops for Murphy's Red or George Killian's Irish Red from the United States.

Porter Porter was developed in 18th-century London and became the most popular style of beer in England. It is a dark-coloured ale made from highly roasted malt that gives it a coffee-like flavour and dryness—a recipe that inspired today's popular stouts (see below). The porter style all but disappeared until small British and American brewers revived the style. In Australia, Sydney's Malt Shovel Brewery makes James Squire Porter and the Lord Nelson brews the seasonal Nelson's Blood. The Wig & Pen makes the seasonal Pass Porter and in Western Australia the Inchant Brewery makes Guildford Porter.

Strong ale Strong ales are diverse in both colour and taste. Generally, they are deep golden to

Richly coloured traditional and boutique-brewery ales provide a tempting alternative for a nation of lager drinkers.

mid-brown in colour with a medium to full body. The warming effect of the higher alcohol is noticeable on the palate. English-origin strong ales often have a malt sweetness and pronounced fruity fermentation characters; bitterness and hop aromas are sometimes evident. The balance of complex flavours is what is important. Old Admiral (6.7 per cent alcohol) is brewed at the Lord Nelson, Ironbrew (7 per cent alcohol) is from Fremantle's Sail & Anchor Pub Brewery and Moonshine is made by Victoria's Grand Ridge Brewery. Old Peculier, made by Theakston brewery in Yorkshire, has a 5.7 per cent alcohol content and is available in Australia. Other popular English imports are Fuller's 1845, Jennings Snecklifter and Morland Hen's Tooth. Scotch ales are another variant with a sweeter malt taste because they are not as fully fermented, leaving unfermented malt sugars. Try the imported McEwan's Scotch Ale from Scotland.

Stout Stouts are made with highly roasted malt. They have a strong roasted, almost burnt, taste and are black in colour. Stouts are very bitter, full-bodied beers. The Guinness brand has spread the taste for stout around the world and the Irish-style pub has come along with it. But as it happens, stout is an abbreviation of stout porter, which, as described above, was originally developed in London in the 18th century. Mr Guinness was the first Irish brewer to copy the English stout porter style. The roasted malts used for brewing stout are prepared in a roaster similar to that used for roasting coffee beans.

Other types of stout include sweet stout (originally called milk stout because milk sugar, or lactose, was used in the brewing), oatmeal stout and imperial stout. Stout brewed with a small amount of oatmeal adds a silky texture and nutty character. Imperial or Russian stouts got their name because they were sent from England to the Russian Imperial Court. They have an alcohol content of up to 12 per cent and more than tease the palate with intense coffee flavours.

Many Australian breweries produce excellent stouts although not in as many variations as the breweries of the UK and Ireland. Most are closer to the dry style and include Carbine (Queensland), Sheaf (New South Wales), Abbotts (Victoria), Southwark and Coopers (South Australia) and Cascade (Tasmania). I've observed that small breweries seem to have an affinity for brewing stouts and they appear regularly on their menus. There's Goulburn Black (Goulburn Brewery), Velvet Cream Stout (Wig & Pen), Irish Stout (Bell's Hotel and Brewery in Melbourne), 'the craic' (Portland Hotel Brewery), Hatlifter Stout (Grand Ridge), Brass Monkey Stout (Sail & Anchor), Robinson's Extra Stout (Sunshine Coast Brewery in Queensland), and Flanagans Dry Irish Stout (Townsville Brewing Co.).

Wheat beer—ale of a kind

Wheat rather than barley gives birth to pale-coloured wheat beers—long popular in Europe and now made in Australia.

Wheat beers, with their top fermentation, belong to the general ale family but given that they are based on a different grain than most beers they deserve to be classified as a separate style of beer in their own right. There are three main varieties of wheat beer, Berlin weisse style, weizen wheat beer from southern Germany, and Belgian white beer.

Weisse style This beer is very pale, acidic, dry, light-bodied, fruity and highly carbonated. Berliner Kindl or Berliner Schultheiss are Berlin's well-known local brews.

Weizen wheat beer is golden in colour, medium-bodied, fruity and clove-like. The weizen style is also made either cloudy or clear. I'd recommend trying Australian Redback Original or Southwark White, which are made in this style. Or look for the German Erdinger or Schofferhoffer, which comes in two versions—the filtered and clear kristall weizen or the unfiltered, yeast-cloudy hefe-weizen.

Belgian white beer This style is very pale and cloudy. It has medium bitterness and body with coriander and orange flavours. Try a drop of Hahn Witbier or Australian White brewed by the Malt Shovel Brewery or look for Belgium's Hoegaarden.

Some brewers add wheat to an ale or lager brew to create new tastes. At Sanctuary Cove in Queensland, the Masthead Brewing Co. makes a specialty wheat beer flavoured with honey, whimsically called Beez Neez. In Western Australia, Darling Range Brewing Company makes a weizen style and the Bootleg Brewery offers Bootleg Wheat. In Victoria, Holgate Brewhouse at Woodend brews White Ale in the Belgian style, and in Sydney the Lord Nelson brews a wheat beer called Quayle Ale.

Lager—how to be very, very popular

In the late 19th century, the rapid development and application of commercial refrigeration in Australia coincided with the arrival of lager beers on the scene. The two were obviously made for each other. Most of Australia's breweries adopted refrigeration at this time and lager's refreshing taste and carbonic bite soon seduced drinkers' palates.

The European lager style was based on an all-malt recipe that delivered a fuller bodied beer with rich flavours. By contrast, the early Australian brewers made use of cane sugar to lighten the body and malt flavour to enhance its refreshing qualities. This lighter style of lager proved a hit in Australia's warm climate. I like the simplicity of the label 'New' for Tooheys most popular lager. It recognises an important development in the history of Australian brewing: 'New' refers to the new lager technology and 'Old', as in Tooheys Old, refers to the traditional ale process.

Mainstream lager Australia's popular lager brands may be taken for granted by local drinkers but they are sought after in many places

Lager: our favourite beer, with a brand for almost every day of the year.

around the world for their bold-flavoured yet refreshing qualities. Most of those beers were designed in the early years of Australia's lager-brewing development. The emphasis on refreshment produced beers that are well rounded in flavour. They are often described as moderate, meaning medium malt, body and bitterness. This doesn't mean moderate in quality: Australia's lagers are made with the best barley malt and hops. XXXX Bitter, James Boag's Original, Tooheys New, Fosters Lager and Swan Draught characterise a regional style of lager known for balancing bitterness with a moderate malt palate. This style is generally less malty than many European lagers, but maltier than American lagers. Other lagers in this category are Victoria Bitter, Southwark Bitter, XXXX Gold, West End Draught, Carlton Cold, Carlton Draught, Emu Bitter, Tooheys Extra Dry, Tooheys Gold, Tooheys Red and West End Gold.

Premium lager These beers are a relatively recent addition to the lager portfolio and have evolved over time. The earliest premiums were premium-packaged beers rather than premium-brewed beers. Nowadays, different malts, special hops—including imported varietal hops—and different processing techniques produce refreshing beers with distinctive flavour highlights. Hahn Premium, Cascade Premium, James Boag's Premium and Southwark Premium are all modern premium lagers with a distinctive taste and refreshing appeal. Crown Lager is a traditional premium lager that has been brewed since the 1950s when it was first produced to celebrate the coronation of Queen Elizabeth. Imported lagers are often thought of as premium beers but in reality some are really mainstream lagers according to the way they are brewed in their country of origin. Popular imported brands, both premium and mainstream, include Heineken, Grolsch, Carlsberg, Stella Artois, Singha, Corona, Tiger, Lowenbrau, Steinlager, Kirin Ichiban, Samuel Adams and Nastro Azzurro (Peroni).

Light beer In Australia, the term 'light' refers to light-alcohol lager brewed with special malt or hop blends to enhance flavour. After years of development with alcohol content as low as two per cent, the Australian style has settled at around 2.7 per cent alcohol. Australian brewers produce both mainstream and premium brands, such as Hahn Premium Light, Cascade Premium Light, XXXX Light Bitter, Fosters Light Ice and West End Light. It is interesting to note that in the United States the term light beer refers to low-calorie beer.

Boutique lager More intense in flavour, these beers often feature all-malt recipes and a high level of hops. They are full-bodied, rich in flavour and invite sipping rather than quaffing. Many of these beers are distinctive and satisfying. There's Scharer's Lager from Scharer's Little Brewery in New South Wales, Buffalo Lager from the Buffalo Brewery in Victoria, and Auroras Lager, hailing from the Auroras Microbrewery in Brisbane.

Pilsener Before refrigeration, Czech brewers were beset by beer going sour in summer so they called in a German brewer to help. Joseph Groll brewed a lager style of beer in the town of Plzen (or Pilsen in English). This lager was different from traditional Munich lager. It had more hop bitterness and a unique pale golden colour. It was so different and had such appeal it quickly became fashionable. Brewers elsewhere soon learned to make pale golden lager to meet consumer demand. We take golden beer as the norm today but it all started in 1842 as pilsener.

Pilsener is a lager but the reverse is not true. Lagers have subtle and delicate flavours whereas pilseners have a rich maltiness and pronounced hop bitterness and aroma, classically derived from Czech hops.

Chuck Hahn
Small breweries, big flavours

My DICTIONARY defines 'small' as—amongst other things—not great in importance. And the expression 'small beer' is said to refer to 'a trifling matter' of 'no importance'. Well, obviously the compilers of that particular volume had never visited a boutique brewery! I've got news for them. As some wise man said back in the 1970s: 'small is beautiful', particularly when it comes to beer. Let me explain.

Small—by brewery standards—copper brewing vessels are a traditional part of small breweries. Malted barley and water are mixed in one vessel for the mashing process. A separate, but equally handsome, copper kettle is used to boil the brew when the hops are added.

At the Malt Shovel Brewery in inner-Sydney Camperdown we've got the best small brewhouse for which any enterprising home brewer could ever wish. While we regularly produce a small range of brands we also have the flexibility to make changes when we want to. Having a beautifully small (excuse me for labouring my favourite point) brewhouse, we have the luxury of experimenting with variety and the occasional delight of coming up with something new, different and exciting.

And we are not alone. From the Little Creatures Brewery in Fremantle to the Mountain Goat in Melbourne and Scharer's Little Brewery in the New South Wales southern highlands, small breweries are producing wonderful tastes. Without the pressure of having to meet the demands of larger volume brands, specialty breweries—I think we all agree it's time to give 'boutique' a break—can add that handcrafted touch to their relatively small batches of ale or lager. For the uninitiated, 'relatively' small means 13,000- or 20,000-litre fermentation tanks as opposed to the 300,000-litre tanks used in larger breweries for major beer brands. The size of our average brew, for example, is likely to be 5000–6000 litres as opposed to 80,000 litres. We brew about six batches only a week and instead of producing a case of cans a second, our bottles rattle off the production line to fill about four cases a minute. And it's music to my ears.

So specialty breweries can not only be beautifully small but also efficiently small. And the experimentation? Well, at the outset they can add more or less malted barley (usually more). They may have small bags of different roasted malts that have been kiln-dried (it's a bit like roasting coffee beans) at different temperatures for varying times. The brewers taste all these fine grains before they brew with them and they taste everything as it's cooked up and fermented.

Later in the crafting process, something described in detail in *How is beer made?* on page 12, the brewer might add as much as three times more hops to the brew than the quantity used in 'standard' beers. We have beers that contain a blend of pale malt from Tamworth in New South Wales and Munich malt from Ballarat in Victoria combined with Czech Saaz and New Zealand Belgian Saaz hops; another beer might have similar malts but combined with many a bagful of English Fuggles hops (for a rich, earthy, floral hop taste); some may be a marriage of wheat and pale barley malt blessed with a generous serve of Williamette hops (an American variety now grown in Tasmania). Not only good to drink but positively multicultural as well!

The end result is distinctive, character-filled flavours that are meant to be savoured more for tastebud stimulation than mere cold-as-you-can-get-it refreshment. Don't get me wrong. Major-brand, high-volume beers are good quality but simpler in structure than our specialty brews.

In the last ten years people have slowly discovered the pleasures of drinking less but tasting more and that's where the small (and beautiful!) small brewery with big-flavoured beers comes in. In the last five years the specialty or premium beer market has doubled while the demand for mainstream beers has been decreasing. As attendances have declined, pubs have responded by providing more interesting beers and serving more inviting food. Many specialty beers are now on tap—they don't just make those handsome little bottles any more, they fill kegs just like the big boys. And different varieties, like wine, combine well with different foods. Remember the three Cs mentioned in *Matching beer with food* on page 63: 'complement, contrast and cut (or cleanse)'. A good beer can cut or cleanse the palate in a way that wine struggles to do with some foods.

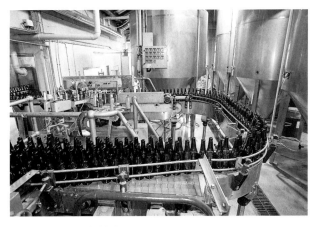

The bottling machine marks the end of the production line—but not always. Many small breweries rely solely on kegs to transport their beer to the thirsty customer.

Join in the spirit of experimentation that inspires our small breweries and drink more beers rather than more beer—and combine them with food. If you haven't tried a small-brewery India pale ale with a fiery Indian curry or a lightly hopped pilsener with your favourite Thai dish then you're not experimenting. Enjoy the experience (you may even have another bottle) and, please, evangelise about beers!

Pilseners are always golden, whereas lagers can be dark in colour from the use of dark malts. Pilsner Urquell is the original pilsener lager and is available in Australia as is Beck's from Germany. A popular brew in this style is Sydney's James Squire Original Pilsener. Other pilseners include Matilda Bay Pilsner (Western Australia), Pilsener 107 (Adelaide) or Tooheys Pils. Pilseners from small brewers include Darling Range pilsener, Wills Pils (Bootleg Brewery), Kiandra Gold Pilsener (Wig & Pen) and Bohemian Pilzner (Masthead Brewing).

Bock This style of beer is a very strong lager. It is copper to brown in colour, full-bodied, high in alcohol, and has a pronounced bitterness. Bock traditionally has an alcohol content of more than 6 per cent. Its more alcoholic sibling, Doppelbock, has an alcohol content of more than 7.5 per cent. I'd recommend trying Burragorang Bock (at 6.4 per cent alcohol) from New South Wales or the seasonal Aviator Doppel Bock (at 7.5 per cent alcohol), from the Wig & Pen. EKU Kulminator from Germany is a classic bock style.

Dark lager This style balances the coffee caramel notes of dark malt with the cleanness of a bottom-fermenting lager process. The style was the everyday drink throughout much of Europe before golden-coloured pilsener became so popular. In Australia, dark lagers are today considered more of a specialty beer. St. Ives Hotel Brewery in Tasmania brews a dark lager called Old Bastard and the Matilda Bay Brewing's Dogbolter special dark lager is available around Australia. In Germany, the Prince of Bavaria still brews a traditional Bavarian dark lager at his small castle brewery. Called Konig Ludwig Dunkel (King Ludwig Dark), it has been exported to Australia from time to time.

American lager The American lager style is light in body and colour with a clean, crisp finish and noticeable carbonation. Often brewed with rice or corn, it has delicate flavours resulting from a low use of hops. Imported brands include Budweiser, Miller and Coors.

Vintage beer—putting something by for later

Vintage beers are usually darker in colour than regular beers, strong in alcohol and designed to be aged for complex flavour development. It takes high alcohol and/or yeast left in the bottle to produce a beer that will age well. These are uncommon beers with strong flavours. Coopers Brewery of Adelaide is one of only a few brewers to have released an annual vintage ale over the last few years. I have had the rare privilege of tasting a 100-year-old vintage ale in England. This Kings Ale was mashed by King Edward VII in February 1902 at the Bass brewery in Burton-upon-Trent. It was bottled with yeast and every 20 years was decanted from sediment, recorked and waxed to ensure its survival. It is a cloudy brown colour with a pungent and complex aroma, and at 11.8 per cent alcohol tastes somewhat like a fortified wine. A classic vintage beer is Belgium's Chimay Blue (called Grande Réserve in the large bottle) which is available at some specialty bottle shops.

Specialty beers—a very individual branch of the family

Characterised by regional traditions, these beers are often produced by brewers dedicated to a particular style. Belgium's lambic beers made with wild yeast are an example. Samuel Adams in the United States makes a 17 per cent alcohol beer that has no carbonation and tastes almost like a port. Unibroue in Canada makes a strong cherry beer that is served hot in ceramic mugs. In France, there is a beer called Adelscott, which is brewed using peated whisky malt to produce a light, smoky taste

Some of the more popular styles of specialty beers have limited availability; specialty styles available in pubs and bars include seasonal Chilli Beer (Sail & Anchor), Bolton's Ginger Beer (Queen's Wharf Brewery in Newcastle), Ginger Kegs (Sunshine Coast Brewery), Auroras Barley Wine and the aforementioned Beez Neez honey wheat beer. The following list is a guide to some of the better known specialty styles brewed around the world.

Altbier This is a dark, light-bodied ale brewed in the Dusseldorf region. It is not generally available in Australia.

Bière de garde These ales from northern France are brewed strong and bottle conditioned with yeast for ageing. La Choulette Ambree is sometimes available locally.

Lambic/kriek These Belgian specialty styles are brewed with wheat using spontaneous fermentation. They have a distinctive sour taste. Kriek is made when brewers add cherries to lambic beer. The fruit sugar begins a slow secondary fermentation and the beer takes on the colour, taste and aroma of the fruit. Other fruits traditionally used are raspberries and blackcurrants. Framboise is a fruit beer in the kriek style brewed with raspberries. Imported brands include Timmermans Kriek and Belle-Vue Kriek.

Kölsch Kölsch is a golden German ale not generally available in Australia.

Trappist ale Now made only in Belgium and the Netherlands, Trappist ales are brewed under the direct control of Trappist monks in just a few surviving monastery breweries. They are bottle conditioned and most can be aged. Chimay, Orval, Rochefort and Westmalle Trappist ales are available in Australia.

Abbey style This style, mainly from Belgium, refers to beer brewed under licence to an abbey by a mainstream brewery and can vary in palate, aroma and colour. Abbey beers are rich and strong but vary

Specialty beers, sometimes aged in the bottle, spring from ancient traditions and may be based on exotic ingredients; with their high alcohol content they are a unique treat and deserve to be relished—something to sip and savour.

widely in taste. Leffe Blonde and Leffe Bruin are available in Australia.

Gueuze This is a blend of lambic beer that has been aged for some years. This style produces very tart, dry characteristics. I recommend trying Timmermans or Belle-Vue Gueuze.

Rauchbier Rauchbier is a smoked beer, a specialty of the Bamberg area of Germany. Some small brewers, particularly in the United States, make this style. The malt is smoked and the smoky flavour comes out in the beer. I have seen the famous Aecht Schlenkerla Rauchbier, which has a taste of smoked ham, in Australia but it is not commonly available.

Bill Taylor

4. The story of beer: from bread to breweries

WHERE did this marvellous and happily ubiquitous drink called 'beer' come from? We know that the word 'beer' comes, appropriately, from the Latin bibere meaning 'to drink'. But long before the ancient Romans put that label on it the drink itself was lubricating social gatherings all over the Middle East. About 6,000 years ago, the Sumerians, who established a very prosperous civilisation in the fertile valleys of the Tigris and Euphrates rivers—part of modern-day Iraq—developed the ancestor of today's beer. By 3000 BC the Sumerians were serious brewers, using an estimated 40 per cent of their cereal production to brew beer. So thanks to these ingenious—and obviously hearty—drinkers, beer can be voted the world's oldest alcoholic drink and the Sumerians hailed as amongst the earliest, if not the very first, promoters of a civilised taste for alcoholic relaxation.

OPPOSITE PAGE: *The concept of combining beer and food is not a new one as the 1940s poster in the background shows. Early beer bottles were similar to the sparkling wine-style bottle on the right and were corked. The 'shouldered' bottle in the centre is from the 1940s while the contemporary shape at left became popular in the 1950s.*

Sumerian beer—sometimes flavoured with honey and dates—was made from cakes of cooked wheat or barley soaked in water and left to ferment. And as proof of how civilised they were, the Sumerians drank their beer in a uniquely fastidious manner, imbibing the thick liquor communally from large earthenware jars through straws made from reeds. Actually they had to do this in order to avoid the husks and other debris from the dissolving cakes of crudely mashed grain, but if you see the earthenware jar as the equivalent of a modern bar—minus the black leather stools—then Sumerian beer drinking certainly stimulated social intercourse and discouraged drinking at home.

ABOVE: *A painting from the ancient tomb of an Egyptian grain merchant, dating from about 1450 BC, records in faithful detail the sowing and harvesting of what appears to be barley—since time immemorial the basis for beer. Photo RMN.*

It all came to an end when the Babylonians invaded Sumeria; luckily the victorious invaders felt that the vanquished Sumerians had hit on something with this beer business. The recipe for beer went back to Babylon with the veterans of the Sumerian campaign and the home population quickly developed a taste for the drink's intoxicating and nutritious effects. Beer became so central to daily life that the Babylonian King Hammurabi introduced special laws governing the sale of beer.

> 'From man's sweat and God's love, beer came into the world.'
>
> ST ARNOLD

For the next few thousand years beer was being discovered independently or handed down from, or copied by, one civilisation after another. As more and more wandering nomads became farmers and herders, grain cultivation became a major occupation that provided not only food but drink as well; a major spin-off preoccupation involved tipping a large part of each crop into large containers of water so that it could ferment. The grains used may have varied from culture to culture but the aim was the same: the production of a successful brew. The Chinese used mainly millet and rice; in tropical and southern Africa it was sorghum and millet; in the Americas, corn; in Europe, wheat, oats and barley.

In ancient Egypt excavations have unearthed plenty of evidence that the Pharaohs and members of the aristocracy were entombed with food and beer to help them on their long journey into the afterlife. Some, perhaps expecting a longish journey and eager to make it a pleasant trip, were buried with as many as 1,000 jars of beer. The health benefits of beer were recorded in the ancient Egyptian medical text, *The Papyrus Ebers*, which lists more than 600 medicinal preparations, more than 100 of them containing beer as an ingredient. The Ebers do not record the popularity or otherwise of these preparations but as the Egyptians brewed beer flavoured with fragrant herbs such as juniper, ginger, saffron and coriander it's unlikely that the unwell who received a prescription required much persuasion to take their daily dose.

Europe, ale, and a new taste sensation

The ancient civilisations may be credited with discovering the brewing process but it was the spread of the Roman Empire that took beer into the heart of Europe and made it the universal drink it is today. Julius Caesar hailed beer as a 'high and mighty liquor' while the historian Pliny the Elder wrote that the Romans and their enemies the Gauls, Visigoths and Vandals would replenish their strength for battle by drinking beer. Who was going to quibble with Julius Caesar, a Visigoth or a Vandal? With endorsements like these, it was inevitable that beer would go 'big-time' in Europe.

By medieval times, beer was well established in those parts of Europe too cool for the growing of a reliable crop of grapes. Europeans were brewing with a vengeance, albeit mostly at home. In England, ale brewing was carried out by women called alewives or brewsters. The best of these home brewers opened up their houses to local drinkers, perhaps pioneering the concept of today's 'local', where people in a neighbourhood gather to enjoy a quiet

Traditional oast houses—used for drying hops—still stand near New Norfolk in the verdant Derwent Valley region of Tasmania.

drink. The production of ale was an important cottage industry long before the establishment of commercial brewing. The English king Alreck of Hordoland is said to have chosen his queen because of her skill at making very good ale.

Even in those days, when life was relatively short and frequently brutal, people had established a link between polluted water and disease even if they didn't understand what the link was; as a result a fermented drink such as beer was often considered safer than water and was drunk by families, adults and children, every day. St Arnold, Bishop of Metz in France, who would have had no inkling of the existence of bacteria, advocated drinking beer instead of water, saying, 'From man's sweat and God's love, beer came into the world'. His wise advice no doubt safeguarded the health of many.

From civilisation's first taste of beer, it would take several millenia for brewers to discover the superiority of the bitter hop as a natural preservative and perfect foil to the drink's sweet malt sugars. In the early centuries of the second millennium, there began to appear in some beers a flavour beyond that of whichever spicy or fruity additive was in favour at the time. The cones or flowers of the hop vine were found to have admirable preservative properties and the brewing monks of central and western Europe started to add them to their beer, as described in *Beer, hops and ... Hildegard*, below. So

BELOW LEFT: *Beer has been brewed in European abbeys since the Middle Ages. The Brewer Monk, from Konrad Mendle's* Chronicle, *1388, showing a monk at work, is the oldest representation of a brewer in Germany.*

Beer, hops and ... Hildegard

Monastery brewers had been experimenting with hops in beer from at least the 8th century but the honour of being the first to record the benefits of hops in beer goes to a woman—and no ordinary woman at that. In 21st-century terms, the Benedictine nun known as Hildegard of Bingen was a trail-blazing feminist who founded her own convent, wrote about herbalism and natural history, composed poetry and music, and in general, rose to such prominence in male-dominated, 12th-century society that she became an advisor to bishops, popes and royalty. At her peaceful convent by the Rhine, near Mainz in central Germany, Hildegard—who has never been canonised but is often described as a saint—oversaw the making of medicinal beers, one of which was flavoured with hops. The result pleased the abbess, who wrote that hops '... when put in beer, stops putrefaction and lends longer durability.' Others felt the same way and beer developed a new, fresh taste that is still with us today.

important was beer and so revered the monks who maintained the brewer's craft, that the Holy Roman Emperor Charlemagne appointed a monk named Gall to oversee monastic brewing across his western European empire. Today this pioneering, multinational brewing executive in a cassock is remembered as St Gall, one of the patron saints of brewing.

Pasteur: the father of modern brewing

The discoveries of the distinguished French chemist and microbiologist Louis Pasteur saved millions of lives. And luckily for the world's beer drinkers his work with microscopic organisms led him to investigate the particular organism to which they owe the pleasure of their drink. Yeast—invisible to the naked eye unless several million cells get together—is the magic ingredient in all alcoholic drinks, consuming sugars and transforming them into alcohol and carbon dioxide. Without yeast, beer would be little more than a cereal cordial; until Pasteur came along brewers sometimes had to throw out whole batches of beer because their impure yeast had multiplied out of control and soured the liquor. Brian Glover, author of the definitive *The Complete Guide to Beer*, doesn't mince words, describing Louis Pasteur as the 'father of modern brewing'. Why? Because Pasteur gave brewers the power to control the most important yet most capricious and unpredictable of their ingredients. In 1876, after several years of research, Pasteur showed that yeast was a living organism that could be contaminated by other micro-organisms. With this knowledge, chemists could isolate a desirable yeast strain, allowing brewers to happily make the most of their yeast with confidence. They've been doing so ever since.

As hopped beer gained in popularity, the lucrative market for other plants and spices used for making ale was threatened; in England, hops were banned for a time and were even called a 'wicked weed' early in Henry VIII's time. But by the time of Henry's death in 1547 drinkers' preference for the cleaner, refreshing taste of hopped beer had won out and the vine was being cultivated in the green fields of Kent. In 1574, English author Reynold Scott reflected popular opinion when he wrote of hops: 'what grace it yieldeth to the taste'.

Taming the wild and wilful yeast

While giving thanks to the many pioneers whose accidental or intentional experimentations gave us beer, they really didn't know what they were doing. In the same way that the average Middle Ages man or woman in the street knew that drinking dirty water was not a good idea without understanding why, early brewers knew that fermentation—a gift from the gods—occurred without realising that they had stumbled upon something called yeast. The gift from the gods was in fact the yeast that, as fate would have it, was carried by the wind onto the infusing liquid, converting the sugars in the immersed grains into alcohol. Various micro-organisms in the storage containers, another unintentional side-benefit of these less than hygienic times, added a lactic sourness. It wasn't until the late 1800s, after Louis Pasteur's work in 1876, that brewers used stable, pure yeast cultures to ferment their ales and lagers. Pasteur's studies on pure yeast, described in *Pasteur: the father of modern brewing*, left, inspired Emil Hansen at the Carlsberg brewery in Denmark to invent an apparatus to grow a pure brewing yeast culture from a single yeast cell. By using pure yeast, brewers were, for the first time, able to consistently produce a pure beer taste. Some European brewers still pay tribute to beer's legacy as a gift from nature by using spontaneous fermentation to make specialty beers like lambic and gueuze. These beers, fermented by wild yeast and bacteria from the atmosphere, taste quite tart and acidic, more like vinegar than modern beer.

Since the turn of the 18th century and the dramatic changes of the Industrial Revolution, science has had a significant influence on how beer is made. Mechanical innovations made large-scale production possible. Breweries began using steam power in the late 1700s and were quick to pioneer the use of thermometers to achieve consistent brewing temperatures and the hydrometer to measure density and thus maintain consistent quality. Steam-powered trains and ships enabled brewers to send their beer further afield. One English beer, still known as imperial stout, got its name because it was sent by ship to the Russian imperial Court; the highly-hopped ale brewed for transportation via the Cape of Good Hope to the thirsty sahibs of the British Raj became known as India pale ales.

A top-to-bottom transformation

But it was the 19th century that brought spectacular change in the brewing industry. Up until then most beers were 'top-fermented'—at room

In Portait of the Artist with his wife Saskia or The Prodigal Son *(1636), Rembrandt, aged 30, painted himself lifting a flute of beer during a playful domestic moment with his wife. The painting is refreshingly lighthearted for a masterpiece.*

temperature the yeast rose to the top of the beer as the malt extract fermented. In the relatively mild climates of central and northern Europe this was only a problem during the short summer months when the yeast sometimes ran out of control and spoiled the brew. Now, one simple but dramatic innovation—the production of a light-coloured beer in the town of Plzen (Pilsen in English) in Bohemia (then part of the Austro-Hungarian Empire, now a province of the Czech Republic) was eventually to alter the way the world thinks of beer.

Sometime in the 1890s, a proud group of maltsters posed with the tools of their trade— and a camera-conscious canine companion—outside Joe White's Maltings in Victoria.

Lager pioneer, Gabriel Sedlmayr, had already developed the art of producing bottom-fermented beers through cold storage at the Spaten Brewery in Munich in the 1830s. But lagers remained dark brown or amber-red like most traditional beers. Then Josef Groll made his first batch of bottom-fermented beer in Plzen and the world's first-ever golden-coloured lager—or pilsener—was born. The pale colour was an accident and probably a result of undercooked barley; despite this, what became known as the pilsener style was copied across Germany, Europe and the world. Today, Pilsener-inspired lagers are the most widely brewed international beers. It didn't take long for beer drinkers to start appreciating the clarity and colour of Plzen's clear, golden pilsener drunk from a glass— Bohemia was famous for its glass making—rather than a tankard.

Ups and downs of an old beer in a new country

Coincidentally, the new colony that eventually was to become known as Australia, was founded at the beginning of the period of the dramatic changes described above. But it would be some time before the new styles and the new technologies coming out of Europe resulted in a beer that we would recognise today taking its place at the public bar. Our first brewer, James Squire, opened his tavern in 1795 and, like his fellow craftsmen in Europe, wouldn't have understood how yeast worked. He would have relied on saving the foam from one brew to make the next. Flavouring beer in the new colony was a problem; hops did not grow well around Sydney, added to which the early brewers were plagued with inferior equipment and hygiene problems. Another pioneer Australian brewer, John Boston, made beer from malted Indian corn that was bittered not with hops but with the leaves and stalks of the love apple or cape gooseberry. It's no surprise that brews of the time were described by such mockingly derogatory names as sheepwash and shypoo, page 111.

So for almost 100 years Australian beer was not the beer we drink today. It was flat top-fermented ale, rather like the flat British beers which, when served at room temperature, bring such a dubious and judgemental reaction when first tasted by visiting Australians in England. And despite the fine efforts by the likes of James Squire and many other brewers who struggled to produce good beer when the best quality ingredients were sometimes hard to find, the local product was often regarded with disdain. Poor ingredients, polluted water, and the summer heat, which encouraged wind-borne bacteria and the yeast to run riot in brewing vats, meant that the brewer's lot was not always a happy one. And there were a lot of potentially unhappy beer makers—any provincial town of a reasonable size had a brewery and between approximately 1860 and 1900 the number of breweries in Australia increased from 178 to 255.

Keith M. Deutsher's encyclopaedic

ABOVE: *The handsome Victoria Inn, one of the finest surviving examples of an 'upper-class' wayside inn, once provided food, drink and shelter for those who crossed the Blue Mountains in NSW. Built of sandstone quarried on site, it stands at the bottom of the Victoria Pass on the busy Great Western Highway between Sydney and Bathurst.*

LEFT: *By the 1920s, horsepower of a modern kind was replacing the traditonal draughthorse.*

> '... the time will surely come when the public in this hot country will demand their ale cold, full of gas, and a long drink for their money.'
>
> THE BREWERS' JOURNAL, 1886

tome *The Breweries of Australia* uncovered no shortage of critics. In 1875 *The Age* in Melbourne trumpeted that Melbourne brewers used green tea leaves, tobacco, acid and various other additives to adulterate their beer. Said the newspaper: '... all over the country suicides, murders, and deeds of violence and brutality are daily occurring under the influence of mania and potu. The working man, who is the largest consumer of beer, as a consequence figures most conspicuously in the gloomy list of tragedies.'

In 1880 a beer-drinking poet lamented, in *The Bulletin*, the after-effects of colonial beer.

> *A pot of beer the beady bubbles breaking;*
> *A hand outstretched to grab the pot and all;*
> *An hour of jollity, a sad awakening;*
> *An awful headache and a taste like gall.*
>
> *An angry wife, in manner all unbending;*
> *A voice, 'You're drunk', a stumble and a fall,*
> *A Yankee broom upon your head descending,*
> *And then you feel your wounds—and that is all*

But in 1890, Mr JC MacCartie, quoted in Cyril Pearl's *Beer, Glorious Beer*, got to the nub of the matter when he produced a spirited defence of local brewers in the aforementioned journal. 'I am tolerably certain,' he wrote, 'that there breathes not a brewer in England at the present time who can come out here and show us how to raise the general character of our product with the present brewing conditions unaltered.' And people were starting to think that perhaps the local style wasn't really appropriate for Australia anyway.

In *A Glass of Ale*, written for Melbourne's Carlton Brewery in 1873 by 'John Barleycorn', the author made a timely comment, in view of the changes that were to

Small beginnings: John Pascoe Fawkner, who built Melbourne's first house and sold beer and 'grog' over a counter at the back prospered sufficiently to later open the Royal Hotel in Flinders Street.

occur in the next decade. Observing that English ales were not suited to the Australian climate he said: 'It is too heavy, too somniferous in its effect for the heat of our summer days, not sufficiently refreshing to the taste, and rather too expensive for universal use. What is wanted to recoup the "waste of tissue", to appease the "drouth" of sun-baked Australians, is a beer that shall be light, yet good: pleasant to the palate, but not unpleasant to the system, a beer, to use a hackneyed quotation, "without a headache in a hogshead of it". Little did Mr Barleycorn know what he was saying—or did he possess a crystal ball?

S T Gill captured the essence of rural, colonial Australia in Sly Grog Shanty (1852). The peaceful scene is not quite all it appears—a 'coffee' sign usually indicated that something comfortably alcoholic was available 'under the counter'.

As if stirred to action by John Barleycorn's observant remarks, Australian brewers made significant improvements to the quality of their ingredients, equipment and brewing skills in the 1870s and '80s. The arrival of refrigeration allowed fermentation and storage temperatures to be controlled and led to widespread lager brewing which was more suited to the Australian climate. According to *Beer, Glorious, Beer*, *The Brewers' Journal*, which had long campaigned for the introduction of a lager beer, was sure that change was on the way when it said in 1886: 'As we have said over and over again beer of the lager type is, in our opinion, the beer of the future, a light, wholesome ... beer, drunk cold and in high condition ... the time will surely come when the public in this hot country will demand their ale cold, full of gas, and a long drink for their money.'

The innovation that was to change the face of brewing in Australia occurred in 1883. *The Breweries of Australia* credits the Sydney Brewery in George Street with being the first Australian brewery to produce lager. The new-style beer was not immediately popular with the drinking public, however lager was here to stay. A succcession of breweries began to brew the new style ... and the rest is history. Among the early successful brewers were Fosters in Victoria and Castlemaine in Queensland—both were selling lager

The real thing: in 1906 the South Australian Brewing Co. installed lager tanks to produce its new König (king) lager. By this time, Australian drinkers were switching their allegiance from traditional ales to lager beers.

by 1889. The new technology was a considerable help of course. Refrigeration not only gave brewers control over temperature—reducing the age-old battle with beer going sour and allowing them to produce beer any time and anywhere—but when installed in pubs it guaranteed that the beer could be served at the temperature the customers preferred.

By the time of Federation, Australians had decided that this new style of beer went rather well with their new country and they have been drinking it ever since. And as the tastes of beer drinkers changed so did the nature of the brewing industry; the 255 breweries in operation in 1900 shrank to 77 by 1920. Under the heading 'A New Era', *The Breweries of Australia* provides a succinct explanation for what happened: 'The beginning of the twentieth century heralded a significant and lasting change in the brewing industry in Australia. New scientific discoveries helped the brewer to understand and control the brewing process in any climate, and the introduction of the lighter lager beer was a more appropriate and preferred beer for Australia … the days of the small-town brewer were disappearing along with the horse and cart.'

In some ways, beer had come full circle—the climate in Australia was more like that of ancient Sumeria than 19th-century Britain; it's nice to think that the Sumerians would have approved of the way the beer was adapted to local conditions. And it's not just the climate; Australian brewers' grains of choice are the same as those used by the Sumerians all those years ago: barley and sometimes wheat.

The new century: a diversity of aromas and flavours

For much of the century after Australians consigned ale to the history books—for the time being anyway—and took lager to their hearts, many drinkers still thought of beer as a one-brand or one-style experience—an effervescent, golden drink consumed ice-cold over the bar or from a tall or squat bottle, often in large quantities and usually with friends. But an increasing number of beer lovers are starting to recognise that the world's oldest drink offers a diversity of aromas and tastes for different occasions and seasons.

... the world's oldest drink offers a diversity of aromas and tastes for different occasions and seasons.

This renewed appreciation of different styles and flavours has stimulated the production of the biggest range of beers ever available in Australia. Thanks to consumers' growing interest in cultural traditions and regional styles from around the world, there are more brewers making premium, boutique and specialty beers. Consumer movements like the Campaign for Real Ale that began in Britain in the 1970s when cask-conditioned beer was in decline, has focused the attention of many drinkers all over the world on an appreciation of what they get when they ask for a 'beer'.

More demand for regional and specialty styles has resulted in wheat beers, traditionally only a summer style in Germany and other parts of Europe, being brewed internationally and drunk all year round. In Australia, discerning beer drinkers looking for different styles and tastes to complement their food can now choose from a wide range of full-flavoured, local premium and boutique beers, as well as imported brands that are available on tap in bars and pubs. In an exciting revival that in a modest way mirrors the growth of breweries in the 1800s, there are now more than 30 microbrewers and brewpubs in Australia, brewing ales, lagers, pilseners, bocks, stouts, porters and their own specialty styles. At the beginning of the 21st century, the choice and quality of beers from brewers large and small has never been better.

Hop vines laden with cones in the foreground and lovingly maintained traditional oast houses in the background make for a scene of idyllic, rural tranquillity at Bushy Park in Tasmania.

Robert Irving

The Australian pub

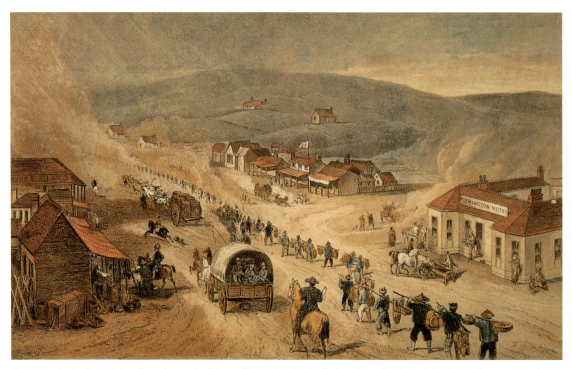

Prominent in the front right of Off to the Diggings, Flemington *by SC Brees (1856)—and prominently placed on the road to entice thirsty diggers—is a public house. At the height of Victoria's gold rush, thousands of goldfields pubs, usually located about a day's journey apart, served the hordes of immigrant diggers.*

IN THE building of its pubs, Australia has been both an inheritor of custom and an innovator of design. British traditions, fused with our unique environments and, more recently, with multicultural influences, make Australian pubs unlike those of any other place.

The styles of our two British models—on the one hand the inn, providing sustenance for travellers, and on the other the tavern or alehouse, catering to local drinkers—were quickly merged, so that most early pubs fulfilled both functions. Licensees of the first public houses were part-timers, with multi-purpose premises. The emancipist William Chapman, who operated The King's Head in The Rocks, was a painter, glazier and butcher, while his wife Ann operated a passenger-boat service to Parramatta, at the same time looking after the pub and a family of nine children. The first roadside inn was The Malting Shovel which catered for the passing trade on the first main road out of the colony, between Sydney and Parramatta. It was licensed to James Squire in 1795. Though initially serving only spirits, Squire was soon brewing beer from locally-grown hops.

In the vanguard

Pubs were among the very first structures to appear in the new settlements dotted around the Australian coast, and they were as diverse as the different local conditions demanded. In Tasmania, like the climate, they were more like those of Georgian Britain. In New South Wales, the heavy summer rains demanded protective verandahs. In Queensland, the sun dictated deep verandahs and shady screens. The Australian pub became not one manifestation but a family of variants. And as towns grew, so pubs changed from simple and fairly primitive structures to more substantial and commodious buildings. They were always social centres— venues for early political movements, theatrical performances, sporting bodies, art, banking, postal services and even church meetings.

Gold ... and its thirsty seekers

The discovery of gold altered Australia forever. In Victoria and New South Wales from the 1850s, in Queensland from the 1860s and 1870s, and in Western Australia several decades later, populations exploded as gold-seekers came, prosperity followed, and new pubs sprang up in their thousands. Pubs near the diggings were simple drinking places. Those in the mining towns responded to the demand for higher standards with better decoration, furnishings, lighting and plumbing, and included such civilised additions as dining rooms and billiard rooms. Railways brought even more people to the growing cities, towns and suburbs. Impressive hotels appeared in gold towns such as Ballarat, Gympie and Kalgoorlie, and of course in the seaboard cities which served them. The ubiquitous verandah, corrugated-iron roof and cast-iron lace decoration were particular Australian features.

The Barmedman Hotel in western NSW was built to take account of an often hot climate; there's shade for customers and passers-by too, and inside, cold beer.

As the Victorian period came to an end, the pub symbolised community success as potently as the town hall, the bank and the church. Furthermore,

The clutter-free, super-streamlined public bar of the Freemasons Hotel in the Sydney suburb of Burwood—brand new when this photograph was taken in 1937—was built to take account of early-closing laws; the bigger the bar the faster the large crowds of peak-hour drinkers could be served.

buildings changed as new technologies evolved with the continuing growth of mechanisation: electricity, cement, pressed metal. The metal structural frame and the passenger lift made tall buildings possible. And while grand city hotels appeared, the epitome of the country pub continued as a wide-verandahed, one- or two-storeyed corner building.

The new century brought Federation and a fresh crop of architectural styles. Pub design changed as reaction against florid Victorian design brought a trend towards simplicity and hand-craftsmanship: for example, cast-iron lace was ousted by timber decoration. But other social forces were at work as well. One was the reduction in the number of hotel licences by Local Option and temperance movements. Another was legislation for six o'clock closing, which followed rioting and looting by several thousand soldiers in Sydney in 1916. Nevertheless, after World War I hotel building resumed. The modern movement brought stainless steel, glass bricks and streamlining. But early closing persisted, and one of its effects was the introduction of longer bars to cater for what the wowsers called the early-closing 'beer swill'.

The pub: a great survivor

Since World War II, the Australian pub has had to respond to further dramatic social changes. The spread of licensed clubs in some states caused a drift away from hotels, though this was modified by the end of early closing. The motel, the hotel-motel and the drive-through bottle shop demonstrated the growing impact of the motor car, and beer gardens abounded. More civilised trading hours, live entertainment, in-house betting facilities, gaming machines, specialty beers and the pub restaurant with international cuisine were other measures which attracted custom. The Australian pub was transformed yet again.

In the last couple of decades the pub has been rediscovered as a powerful and attractive part of Australia's history, with heritage values that are being enhanced and popularised by careful conservation.

Bill Taylor

5. Matching beer with food

STRAWBERRIES and cream. Fish and chips. Horse and carriage. Love and marriage ... beer and food. It is as natural and inevitable a pairing as the other four—and a very happy marriage beer and food make too. After all, they have a common ancestry, with beer beginning as a fermented porridge way back in ancient Sumeria. Some hungry and thirsty or simply curious soul tasted the unlikely brew and we have to assume that after a sip or two he or she felt more than pleased with the result for beer has been one of the world's most popular tipples ever since.

As for matching food with beer—it's not difficult. It's largely a matter of personal preference. In the same way that most beer drinkers know the type of beer they prefer at any given time of day, there is a beer to be paired with almost any food as long as you think the combination works. The two can be mixed and matched to bring out the best in each other—especially if you follow a few simple guidelines.

With food, the visual appeal on the plate and the first aromas are enjoyed before the 'mouthfeel', or texture, the actual taste, and the aftertaste. Beer is enjoyed in exactly the same way. The sensory enjoyment of beer is a combination of taste, aroma, mouthfeel and the liquid's presentation.

ABOVE: *In its home country delicate sushi, like this one from Toko, Paddington, is often matched with an elegant light beer such as Kirin Ichiban lager.*

PREVIOUS PAGE: *Timmermans framboise, a tart, fruity beer that makes a wonderful aperitif or dessert drink, is fermented with wild yeast before raspberries are added for a secondary fermentation. Match it with fresh berries and desserts.*

Making the best of a great match

So beer and food are a great match but are we making the best of the many possible combinations? With the popularity of cool, refreshing lagers in our part of the world, beer has been most commonly associated with casual eating and pre-dinner drinking. But beer is a versatile drink and it would be a great shame to dismiss it from the dinner table. With the almost endless variety of beers available today it's possible to find a beer to suit every occasion, every mood, and most importantly, every food. In fact one of the most enjoyable aspects of beer is the pleasure to be found in pairing it with good food.

Some writers make pairing wine with exactly the right food sound downright daunting but pairing beer and food is a relatively straightforward matter, and it's more affordable! Individual palates and preferences vary, but I agree entirely with the approach summed up succinctly by Lucy Saunders in *Cooking with Beer*. She says that 'cut', 'complement' and 'contrast' are the 'three Cs' of any food and beverage pairing. I have certainly put this rule to good use with beer. Here are some examples of how to follow the three Cs.

Cut (or cleanse) The assertive bitterness of an Emu Bitter or a James Squire Original Pilsener cuts through a rich cheese or a korma curry, cleansing and reviving the palate. A crisp, bitter Peroni lager cuts through creamy pasta dishes.

Complement Oysters, in their various and delicious culinary guises, are a good example of a food that is well complemented by a variety of different beers. The clean, crisp, dry taste of a Tooheys Extra Dry complements the fresh taste of natural oysters. The citrus tartness in a Hahn Witbier (wheat beer) complements oysters dressed with balsamic and lime. A Tooheys Old, with its roasted flavour, best complements the grilled flavours of smoky bacon and worcestershire sauce in oysters kilpatrick. The easiest way to remember how to complement is to remember to select like with like. Choose mild beers with mild food, robust beers with robust dishes and spicy, hoppy beers for the hot and fiery.

Contrast The bitter roasted intensity of a Guinness or Murphy's stout is a fine contrast to natural oysters—a combination made famous by the Irish. A cold Tooheys New provides a stimulating contrast to a barbecued lamb kebab, whereas a Tooheys Old would complement the same dish.

Among the many local beer and food matches I have enjoyed all over the world some stand out: a rich and fruity English ale with roast beef or beef Wellington is a classic match; the delicate Japanese Kirin Ichiban lager is a

Choose mild beers with mild food, robust beers with robust dishes and spicy, hoppy beers for the hot and fiery.

Belgian-style witbier, brewed with orange and coriander, is the perfect foil for salty seafoods—especially those served with lime or lemon.

Fruit cake, suprising as it may seem, is complemented by the fruit flavours in ale. Robert Castellani's mother-in-law created this cake with porter, page 136.

perfect partner to sushi; the aromatic Singha lager from Thailand is superb with fragrant Thai food; the crisp, bitter Spendrups Old Gold lager from Sweden goes well with salty herrings; a full-bodied Munich lager is perfect with pork chops and sauerkraut; the full-bodied and bitter Tiger lager of Singapore is wonderful with chilli crab. Most of these combinations work well because they complement the food.

But there is no need to go overseas for inspiration. You will find plenty of inspiration in the local recipes using local ingredients within this book (all of them created to be cooked with, or accompanied by, beer). Whitebait, parsley and pancetta fritters are perfect to eat with a bitter lager. Spiced grilled chicken with a green salad goes well with a robust ale. Mother-in-law's cake made with spices and dried fruit is cooked with porter as well as served with it. Chicken is braised in ale, prawns in lager and crab is braised with black beans, chilli and ale. Complement the dish perfectly by drinking the same type of beer as used in the cooking.

Why beer belongs on the table

Beer and wine share many of the same attributes as an accompaniment to food. Both are based on an agricultural crop and yeast fermentation with a resulting complexity of flavour. Both can be dry or sweet, full-bodied or thin. They have a moderate acidity. Both have tannin and can be astringent. Wine is still or sparkling while beer is mostly sparkling. Beer has a bitter dryness and arguably a wider range of different tastes. Both contain alcohol though beer is generally the more moderate drink. Given all that the two have in common it is easy to see that beer can be as natural a food partner as wine.

Is beer good for you?

Modern doctors and scientists are confirming what the ancient Egyptians believed such a long time ago: beer is good for you. Moderate alcohol consumption, whether beer or red wine, has a positive effect on the cardiovascular system and some studies have even shown that moderate drinkers live longer than teetotallers! This may come as a surprise to our modern minds but if we think of beer as our ancestors did—an extract of grain seasoned with herbs and fermented by nature—perhaps we should see it as a 'natural' drink with many health-giving qualities. After all, beer contains B vitamins, minerals, folate, fibre and antioxidants, and its most common seasoning, the hop, has increasingly become a source of interest to health scientists.

PS: Beer is not fattening—it has fewer kilojoules than milk, fruit juice and wine. Not only is there no fat in beer, there is no sugar left after fermentation. Just go easy on the salty and fatty nibbles and remember, moderation.

Beer and spice It must be said that there are some flavours that beer is uniquely able to partner—spicy food and chocolate are the stand-out examples. I love the fragrant aromas of spicy Thai, Malaysian or Indian cooking and they combine perfectly with dry, aromatic, hoppy lagers. The layers of flavour in the beer seem to mirror those in the food. The aromas tantalise. There is sufficient body and flavour in the beer to marry with the taste of the food and the lingering heat of the spice is matched by the lingering bitterness of the lager. The alcohol gradually dissolves the heat as the bitterness and the chill on the beer cools and revives the palate. Definitely proof of a marriage of flavour, not a flirtation! For more detail about this spicy marriage see *Beer and spice* by Carol Selva Rajah on page 118.

... complement the dish perfectly by drinking the same type of beer as used in the cooking.

Beer and chocolate Sometimes I think stout was created especially for chocolate. It is a magic combination and an absolute indulgence. The good news these days is that scientists are reporting that both chocolate and stout can be beneficial to your health so we can enjoy them guilt-free—always in moderation of course!

I once presented a master-class on beer and food matching with well-known Brisbane chef, David Pugh. We served a valhrona chocolate dessert with Carbine stout as the finale. David admits he has found it almost impossible to find a wine to match chocolate. Stout seems to be the perfect solution.

Stout deserves to be better known as a dessert beer—it is delicious combined with a chocolate dish. George Diamond's Dark valhrona chocolate tart is on page 133.

When serving stout with dessert it is definitely best presented in glass flutes. While I enjoy rich chocolate cake, I often serve just plain chocolate-dipped strawberries with flutes of stout. Many people, particularly women, have told me they like this combination having previously been turned off by stout served in large, pub-style glasses. So remember, presentation counts!

The flavour of stout is complex and intense. In it there are chocolate, coffee, liquorice, pepper, nutmeg, roasted and bitter flavours which harmonise with the chocolate. The bitterness in a good chocolate makes the unique match complete. I also enjoy the textural synergy—stout and chocolate both have a smooth feel in the mouth. This physical combination, the unique bitter interaction and the sharing of chocolate flavours is a multilayered harmony all of its own.

Organising a beer dinner

When I plan a beer dinner I like to arrange it so that the flavour progresses through the meal. I tend to start with beers that leave the palate fresh such as a lager or pilsener served in a tall elegant glass which gives the beer a generous dense foam. Light or mainstream lagers are good for this. They are a great aperitif—they sharpen appetites and relax the guests. In winter, I choose more robust and nourishing flavours; try Tooheys Pils with 5.2 per cent alcohol or a German Beck's.

With a light and delicate seafood appetiser such as scallops, I match a clean, crisp, dry beer—Tooheys Extra Dry or Hahn Premium Light.

Maggie Beer's mother-in-law perfected the light, crunchy batter used for Flathead in beer batter, page 93. The secret? Make it the day before.

Going onto the starter means moving up in flavour—with a Thai chicken salad I would pair a Belgian-style witbier (wheat beer) such as Hahn or Hoegaarden brewed with coriander and orange peel. A hoppy Australian premium beer would also work well—James Boag's Premium and Hahn Premium are both appropriate. With tea-smoked trout the smoky caramelised flavour of a Tooheys Old partners well. For a spicy pasta or noodle dish the well-hopped XXXX Bitter would be ideal.

With a main course of beef or lamb I serve full-flavoured darker ales such as James Squire Amber Ale or Theakston Old Peculier from the UK. I prefer these beers served slightly warm in wine glasses to allow the guests to fully appreciate the aromas. Ales are ideal with hearty winter food such as casseroles, while lagers and pilseners are perfect in summer with fish and shellfish, chicken and salads.

Desserts and beer surprise some guests. Again, sticking to the three Cs rule, I look for complementary flavours. A raspberry crusted brûlée is superb with a flute of sharp, acidic Belgian framboise. A goblet of James Squire Porter is an excellent match for a small caramel pecan tart. Southwark Old Stout is wonderful with chocolate mud cake. A flute of Hahn Witbier superbly matches a Grand Marnier soufflé or try a pale ale with cheesecake.

I also love beer with cheese. Stouts such as Southwark or Cascade are a delight when combined with a pungent blue or smoked cheese, while a pale ale perfectly matches a cloth-wrapped, matured cheddar. The yeasty bite of some cloudy ales is good with a ripe brie and the bitter Pilsner Urquell is well suited to a sharp, salty fetta. My fellow beer lover Richard Thomas, see *Cheese and beer marriages*, page 134, may challenge some of these combinations but as I said at the outset, it's largely a matter of personal taste.

A cleansing ale is renowned as a digestif. The carbonation massages the palate helping to revive it after a long meal. The chill refreshes and the crisp bitterness stimulates the taste buds. And there are other ales to choose from: a glass of 9 per cent-alcohol Chimay Blue is akin to having a port or a brandy and can be served in a balloon glass. A Southwark Old Stout provides a relaxing influence after a meal while the boutique beer, Burragorang Bock, settles the stomach. And as for the strong English ale, Riggwelter, it encourages a quiet contemplative mood. Such choices take beers beyond the realm of mere refreshment.

Flavour highlights When planning a menu for a beer dinner look for opportunities to add highlights in flavour to link the food and the beer. This is one of the good things about eating at home. When cooking roast beef add some caramelised onions, roast sweet potato and perhaps some fruit chutney and this will align with the roasted and fruity flavours found in a dark ale. When putting a cheese platter together add some quince paste, dried muscatels, figs or dates to enhance the interesting flavour chemistry that occurs when the cheese is matched with a fruity pale ale.

A wedge of lime served with seafood fits well with a clean, crisp, dry beer. The sting of wasabi with sushi works with delicately bittered Ichiban. It is not always the main ingredient that makes the match a success. It may be the sauce, the marinade, the herbs or spices that lift it from the ordinary to something memorable. For further examples of beer and food pairings see *Serving beer with food*, page 71 and *Beer and food matches*, page 72.

The sting of wasabi with sushi works with delicately bittered Ichiban. It is not always the main ingredient that makes the match a success.

At meal's end, a small glass of strong beer proves a soothing restorative that encourages a philosophical contemplation of the simple delights of food and beer at the table.

Cooking with beer

Cooking with beer or cuisine à la bière is the next step for lovers of food with beer. The use of beer in cooking must surely have begun from earliest times when beer was the main drink available to all ages. Beer was created by many different races and brewed from a variety of cereals—wheat, oats, rice, millet, maize and sorghum. It's reasonable to assume that when beer was readily at hand and water may have been unsafe, that beer very readily found its way into the pot for braising and poaching, as a flavour additive, or into dough as a leavener and flavour in baking breads and cakes.

There are traditional recipes for cooking with beer in most northern European countries but it is in Belgium and northern France that cuisine à la bière is a classic style of cooking. *Carbonnade à la flamande* is beef slowly braised in a strongly hopped beer with onions and bread. Fish is poached in beer, and mussels are steamed open in beer and served with the resulting beer and mussel liquid. Beer is used in many cures for ham in Germany. In Ireland, porter or stout flavours and moistens a spicy fruit cake. In Australia, many cooks prefer a beer batter for frying fish, and steak and kidney pie cooked with ale is a well-known favourite. As we become more adventurous in sampling the many new varieties of beer now available it makes sense to use them in the kitchen.

Beef carbonnade is one of the great classics of cuisine à la bière. Janni Kyritsis' mouth-watering version of this dish is inspired by a dish he enjoyed in Paris, see page 125.

The golden rules for cooking with beer

• Use a good-quality beer with a good flavour that you like to drink. A stale or inferior beer won't taste any better when used as an ingredient.
• More is not better. Resist the temptation to use more beer than is suggested in the recipe—beer is a subtle enhancement. The beer often integrates with the other flavours and so is not tasted as beer.
• Use like with like—a light delicate beer with delicate dishes and robust beer with hearty food. Remember 'complement' from the three Cs.
• Time the addition of the beer. Some beers are very strongly flavoured and

the bitterness will concentrate in the dish rather than evaporate. Sometimes I add just a tablespoon of amber ale per cup to minestrone a minute or two before removing it from the heat to ensure a 'bright' flavour balance.
• Follow the instructions—the authors of the recipes have taken account of all the 'rules' listed here.

Those who love beer and those who love food and cooking will find that matching beer and food offers opportunities for some innovative culinary adventures. As we move to lighter foods and a healthier approach to cooking and eating, the growing interest in beer is relevant and timely.

Serving beer with food

Are there any short cuts to establishing which beer style goes with a particular food? As with wine and food, there are many fine beer-food combinations and it's not difficult to become familiar with them. Some of these are marriages made in heaven like the previously mentioned mussels cooked in lager and beef stewed in an amber ale. But a dish doesn't have to be cooked in beer to make beer the ideal drink to accompany it. As mentioned before, the key is to match the amount of flavour in the beer to the amount of flavour in the food: light beer with light food and vice versa. Simply ensure that neither the beer nor the food overwhelms the other—ideally they should be better in combination than apart.

A lightly spiced chicken or prawn dish goes well with a dry style of light lager. Hearty meat dishes need a complex beer like an amber ale or a porter to complement the richness. Stout and porter are ideal accompaniments to some desserts.

Matching cheese with beer can be fun—an old-fashioned ale is the perfect accompaniment to a sharp, mature cheddar.

Be adventurous. The range of beer available in small bottles makes experimenting easy. There are endless partnerships to explore. Look for both contrast and harmony within the bounds of the golden rule of matching the strength of flavour in each.

The suggestions over the page aim to provide the inspiration for a culinary adventure in the world of tantalising and sometimes magical flavour combinations. For further beer brand names refer to *Styles of beer*, page 36.

Beer and food matches

Asparagus and artichokes Almost any lager is acceptable.

Beef Full-bodied malty ales are ideal. Darker ales are excellent with char-grills—try amber ale, dark ale or even porter. Full-bodied, rich-tasting ales are best.

Dried beans and peas Crisp lager and pilsener styles with some malty sweetness are a good match.

Cheese The wide variety of cheese available can be partnered with beer, from pilseners and pale ales to dark ales and stout. See also *Cheese and beer marriages*, page 134.

Chicken and pork The beer may vary according to preparation. Drink a moderately bitter and malty lager with roasted and barbecued chicken and pork. Try a light, dry-style lager with poached chicken.

Chilli con carne and chilli-hot dishes Drink a bitter lager or bitter pilsener.

Desserts Fruit pies and tarts go well with fruity top-fermented ales; fruit cake appreciates a strong dark ale or a porter; chocolate desserts go well with porters and stouts; pair caramel desserts with amber ales; and try fresh fruit with amber ales. Belgian fruit beers, such as kriek, are a delightful surprise with gelato and some iced desserts.

Duck and quail Try a mellow top-fermented ale such as Tooheys Old. Orange sauces work well with fruity ales—try James Squire Amber Ale.

Fish Fried fish goes well with a dry-style light lager; grilled or barbecued fish needs a full-strength, well-hopped lager, dry lager or a premium lager.

Ham A crisp lager like XXXX Gold is well suited to ham though stronger styles such as proscuitto need a malty bitter pilsener such as Pilsner Urquell.

Lamb Roast lamb likes a mellow, pale or amber ale; barbecued or grilled chops prefer a bitter cleansing lager or a darker ale; casseroles need a rich, malty pilsener or an ale.

Oysters natural Try a dry, lightly hopped lager such as Tooheys Extra Dry or Carlton Cold. Keep the bitter lagers and pilseners for oysters with chilli and a dark ale like Tooheys Old for oysters kilpatrick.

Paella A full-flavoured lager such as Tooheys New, XXXX Bitter or West End Draught.

Pasta The beer will depend on the sauce. See also

The Germans long ago learned how to combine beer with food, even if it's just a homely dill pickle and a freshly baked pretzel.

seafood, cheese and beef suggestions. Try a moderately hopped lager with tomato and meat sauces. A bitter pilsener is a refreshing counterbalance to a creamy sauce.

Pickled or smoked fish and meats Tart Belgian lambic beers are good palate cleansers with heavily smoked foods. Dark roasted lagers or ales are a good complement—try Dogbolter or James Squire Porter. Pickled fish is good with thirst-quenching, moderately bitter lagers like Tooheys Maxim or XXXX Gold.

Pizza Generally, mainstream lagers are favoured, try

Tooheys New, Carlton Draught or XXXX Gold Lager.

Quiche and egg dishes Malty, lightly bittered lagers such as Tooheys Extra Dry and Carlton Cold.

Salads Light-bodied beers with delicate malt and hops are preferred—Tooheys Maxim and Hahn Premium Light.

Sausages Generally it depends on the style of sausage. Mainstream lagers for standard sausages; spicy or aromatic sausages need a hoppy beer like Cascade Premium or Hahn Premium; honey-flavoured pork sausages taste good with a fruity Tooheys Old or a crisp malty Tooheys Pils.

Shellfish A moderately hopped lager or fuller malty lager depending on the intensity of shellfish flavour.

Soups The beer may vary according to the ingredients. Look at the fish and cheese suggestions. For vegetable soups try a lager; for meat and herb-flavoured soups choose an ale. Beer soups? Yes—drink the same beer as in the soup!

Spicy food This is where beer comes into its own. There is a wide variety of choice depending on the ingredients and cooking method. For subtle dishes lagers are recommended. As the heat intensity and complexity of the flavours increase, choose hoppy, full-bodied, bitter lagers. Malty bitter pilseners are excellent 'fire' quenchers. Consider wheat beers like Hahn Witbier or Hoegaarden with fragrant Thai dishes. See also *Beer and spice*, page 118.

Sushi Choose lightly hopped lagers. The clean crisp finish of Japanese lagers are ideally suited—Kirin Ichiban is perfect.

Terrines and pâtés A rich ale such as James Squire Amber Ale or Kilkenny red ale is good. For contrast a light lager as a palate freshener can be fun.

Veal A malty lager is a good match.

Vegetable dishes Lightly coloured and flavoured lagers are excellent with green vegetables; move to the amber ales for roasted root vegetables; drink light-bodied dark ales like Tooheys Old with char-grilled vegetables.

A beer for wine drinkers

I once attended a wine festival in northern Bavaria where grain and grapes grow closely together. As I sat at a large table I saw many people drinking steins of beer with their bratwurst and potato salad. Throughout the afternoon small glasses of different wine styles were served to toast the Gewurtztraminer harvest, the Muller Thurgau harvest and so on. When I asked a local about the reason for serving beer at a wine festival he replied that they enjoyed the best of both worlds—they knew that they couldn't drink wine all day. So, for wine drinkers, here is another way to look at drinking beer, eating with beer or even cooking with beer.

If you are used to drinking wine but feel like a beer then this list is for you. While beer doesn't taste like wine the flavour structures in beer can appeal to wine drinkers as much as their favourite fermented grape drink.

Chardonnay Try the hoppy fragrance and bitter dryness of a pilsener.

Sauvignon Blanc Try an aromatic, fruity top-fermented pale ale or the German kristall weizen style.

Riesling The fruity dry taste of a fragrant, hoppy premium lager is appealing.

Semillon The fruity complexity of a yeasty pale ale is worth a try.

Sparkling white The acidity and fruity effervescence of a Belgian-style white (wheat) beer is refreshing.

Sparkling burgundy Try the tart fruitiness of a Belgian kriek (fruit) beer.

Merlot Sample the light fruitiness and mellow malt of an amber ale.

Shiraz Experience the dry, mouthfilling spiciness of India pale ale.

Cabernet sauvignon Taste the complexity of a stong, dark, fruity English ale.

Pinot Noir Look for a mellow, dry brown ale.

Botrytis riesling Try a sweet, malty, scotch ale.

Port A bottle of aged, spicy, sweet Belgian Trappist ale is worth a try.

Alan Saunders
Contemporary watering holes

THERE'S a pub in Sydney (perhaps it had better remain unnamed) which some time ago underwent a makeover intended to make it look old. This was odd, because, until then, it had looked really old. The trouble was, though, that it used to look old in a shabby, familiar sort of way. So where once the place was cluttered with lots of big comfy armchairs with upholstery that didn't match, there are now pool tables, bar stools and glass pictures intended to evoke the 1920s. All this and a big, metallic, art-deco thing over the bar. It's an Australian equivalent of all those English pubs in which, one suspects, genuine oak beams have been torn out and replaced by plastic imitation oak beams.

Gloriously bedecked in cast iron, the Bellevue Hotel was one of the last of Brisbane's distinctive 19th-century watering holes— until it fell, after a long and loud public battle, to a government-sponsored, post-midnight wrecker in April, 1982. Photographed by JM Freeland.

What happens to the old locals when their favourite watering hole undergoes this sort of transformation? Probably what happens is that they turn up once after the decorators have left but never come back. I have seen an old man, shabbily dressed, standing in the middle of an inner-city pub a day or two after it had reopened with bare, polished floorboards and designer beer. He was staring ahead at nothing in particular. He looked completely lost.

The point about places like this is that they are pubs that aspire to the status of bars. There are lots of pubs like this and there are recognised ways of achieving the transformation: you change the floors (polished boards or bare concrete), you bring in some new furniture (low and plastic or perhaps chromium if you're going for a retro look), you beef up the bar menu with noodles and a mezze plate, and, if you're feeling really ambitious, you tack on a restaurant. Outside you post a large man in black without a neck who may be a bouncer, may be a security guard or could, perhaps, be an officer of the style police.

This is indicative of one of the chief characteristics of drinking places in the early 21st century: you simply cannot go by names any more. Just because the Yellow Pages describe it a pub, don't think it can't be a bar. And just because it's called a bar, don't always expect it to be a place where you are served alcohol: not only are there booze-free coffee bars, sushi bars and pasta bars, but there are even unlicensed places calling themselves tapas bars that buck Hispanic tradition and will serve you neither a glass of sherry nor a San Miguel beer.

Boundaries are fluid these days. There are pubs with good cocktail lists and respectable selections of boutique beers, but, if you're really uncertain as to what sort of establishment you've stumbled into, it's worth remembering that a lot of bars either have good views or are underground, which is almost never the case with pubs, that pubs don't offer table service and that bars don't usually contain pokies or TV screens. (One of the curious things about the pub TV is that it's always turned on. It's usually showing sport but it could be showing *Hamlet* and they'll still have it on, even though the place is so loud that you can't hear a single soliloquy. The idea, presumably, is that anything, however inaudible—Shakespeare, current affairs or a British sitcom that never went to a second series—is preferable to the dead stare of a blank screen.)

Anybody interested in the marriage of food and beer has reason to be thankful not only to pubs but to bars as well and to the dialectic between the two. On the one hand, it was pubs that brought us boutique beers: genuine boutique beers, produce of small breweries or small corners of large breweries, not just flavourless, light-shot bottles from Mexico. On the other hand, it was bars that (pardon the pun) raised the bar as far as food was concerned. If it wasn't for bars, pub food would still be all about pies, limp salads and having to take a little flag with a number on it back to your table so that the waiter knows how to find you when he turns up with your crumbed fish and chips. There's little sense in drinking beer with your food if the food isn't worth eating, and bars have widened the choice and made life more interesting even for people who wouldn't be seen dead in one or wouldn't be let in even if they wanted to be.

What a pub looks like after a renovated bar has raised the bar: the Paddington Inn, Sydney.

6. Light touches: snacks and starters

Stefano Manfredi, bel mondo

Crostini with peas, roast garlic and anchovies

Although this is a canapé, I regard it a little like comfort food on crostini. The sweetness of the peas and the roast garlic contrasts well with the bite of anchovies, providing a nice foil for a malt-honey and hop-bitter pilsener.

1 Roast the whole garlic heads on a baking sheet in a preheated oven at 120°C for 30–45 minutes until they are soft. Cut the heads in half and squeeze the garlic out like toothpaste into a bowl. Mash with a fork, then mix in the olive oil and the anchovies. Season to taste and mix thoroughly.
2 To make the crostini, brush your favourite bread with olive oil. Arrange on a baking sheet and bake in a preheated oven at 200°C for 10 minutes until lightly toasted. Spoon a little of the garlic and anchovy mix on each piece of toast, finish with some peas and parsley on top and serve.

4 garlic heads, left whole
6 tablespoons extra virgin olive oil
6 anchovy fillets, chopped into small pieces
Salt and freshly ground black pepper
10 thin slices of good bread
Olive oil
2 cups freshly shelled peas, blanched
½ cup finely chopped fresh flat-leaf parsley

Serves 8–10 as a canapé

Gary Miller, Christchurch Casino

Coconut chutney

Serve this refreshing dip with curries as well as your favourite flat bread.

1 Place the coconut, chillies, ginger and salt in a food processor. Blend until it is a smooth paste. Stir the yoghurt into the coconut paste and reserve.
2 Heat the oil over a medium heat in a frying pan, then add the mustard seeds and curry leaves. As the seeds begin to pop add the coconut-yoghurt paste, turn the heat down and cook for 5 minutes, stirring a couple of times. Remove from the heat and allow to cool before serving.

2 cups grated fresh coconut or shredded coconut
2 green chillies, deseeded, roughly chopped
2 tablespoons fresh ginger, sliced
Pinch of salt
3 tablespoons natural yoghurt
2 tablespoons vegetable oil
1 teaspoon mustard seeds
10 curry leaves

Makes about 2 cups

LEFT: *Stefano Manfredi's Crostini with peas, roast garlic and anchovies.*

David Sampson, Lynwood Stores
Welsh rabbit

While this dish is well-known, not many know it was traditionally served after rabbit hunts in the UK. If topped with a poached egg it became a golden buck. Serve with the same porter that went into the pot—that's traditonal too!

80 g butter
¾ cup flour
1¼ cups milk, hot
¾ cup porter, hot
2 teaspoons tabasco
2 tablespoons Worcestershire sauce
2 tablespoons English mustard
Pinch cayenne pepper
300 g cheddar cheese, grated
2 teaspoons salt
2 teaspoons freshly ground black pepper
3 egg yolks
Sourdough bread

Serves 10, 2 slices each

1 Melt the butter in a saucepan over a medium heat and stir in the flour. Keep stirring until amalgamated. Add the hot milk and porter and stir slowly until it is a thick sauce. Turn the heat to a simmer and cook for about 30–40 minutes.

2 Add the tabasco, Worcestershire sauce, mustard and cayenne pepper to the milk-porter mixture. Cook for a further 10 minutes then add the grated cheese and season with salt and pepper. Do not allow to boil. Let cool then beat in the egg yolks. Refrigerate for 3 hours.

3 To serve, slice the sourdough and toast lightly on both sides. Smooth some rabbit mixture on top with a palette knife. Place under a preheated hot grill until golden brown. Serve immediately.

Gary Miller, Christchurch Casino
Muhammara

A red capsicum, walnut and pomegranate dip with spicy overtones.

6 red capsicums
2 tablespoons olive oil
4 tablespoons walnuts
½ teaspoon chilli
2 tablespoons ground cumin
1 tablespoon paprika
2 tablespoons sugar
1 tablespoon pomegranate concentrate or lemon juice

Makes about 2 cups

1 Cut the capsicums into quarters and remove the seeds, core and ribs. Lay them skin side up on an oiled baking tray and roast in a preheated oven at 200°C until the skin is blistered. Place them in a plastic bag for 10 minutes. Remove the skin and discard. When cool, place the capsicums in the food processor with the other ingredients and purée. Serve with flat bread.

Joan Campbell, *Vogue Entertaining and Travel*

Beer battered zucchini flowers with goat's cheese

A visual delight to serve as a starter washed down with a cold lager.

1 To make the batter, combine all the batter ingredients and blend well in a food processor or blender. Allow to stand for 30 minutes.
2 To stuff the flowers, remove the stamens from the zucchini flowers. In a bowl combine the cheese, olives and pepper and stuff the base of each zucchini flower with a teaspoon of the mixture.
3 To deep-fry the flowers, pour the vegetable oil into a deep fryer or a large saucepan to ⅓ of the depth. Bring to the boil over a high heat. When a breadcrumb colours within 1 minute it is the correct temperature. Dip 1 or 2 flowers at a time in the batter. Shake off the excess and drop the flowers into the oil to fry until golden. Lift out with a slotted spoon, drain on absorbent paper and serve.

Batter

2 cups flour
1 cup lager (more if necessary)
3 eggs, beaten
Pinch of salt
1 tablespoon olive oil

Stuffing

Zucchini flowers (2–3 each depending on size)
125 g goat's cheese
2 tablespoons pitted and chopped olives
Freshly ground black pepper

Vegetable oil for frying

Serves 4–6

Sue Fairlie-Cuninghame, *Inside Out*

Fast beer soup

A nice comforting soup for cold days.

1 Put the lager and sugar into a large saucepan over a medium heat and stir occasionally until the sugar is dissolved. Bring to the boil and then remove from the heat.
2 Whisk the egg yolks in a bowl until mixed but not frothy. Then whisk in the sour cream, a spoonful at a time. Stir a ladle of the hot beer into the egg and cream mixture and then, whisking continuously, pour the egg and cream into the hot beer. Season with cinnamon, salt and pepper to taste. Return the soup to a low heat and cook for a few more minutes until the soup thickens. Do not allow it to boil or it will curdle. Serve in warm bowls with the buttery croûtons.

3 x 345 ml bottles fresh lager or beer of choice
2½ tablespoons sugar
5 large fresh egg yolks
125 ml sour cream
Fresh ground cinnamon to taste
Sea salt to taste
Freshly ground black pepper to taste
Croûtons (small pieces of bread fried in unsalted butter)

Serves 4

Peter Doyle, Celsius
Spicy green olives

These tempting olives provide a little blast with drinks to awaken the appetite. Serve with crusty bread and a small bowl of diced preserved lemon peel to balance the flavours. Accompany with your favourite pilsener. These two recipes are from my book Golden Flavours of Summer.

1 To prepare the olives, drain them from their brine and rinse. Put them in a container, add the remaining ingredients, place the lid on and shake to mix well. Leave the olives to marinate for a few hours or refrigerate until needed. Return to room temperature before serving.

1½ cups picholine or firm green olives
1 garlic clove, minced
1 red serrano or similar hot chilli, seeded and finely chopped
1 teaspoon coriander seeds, lightly crushed
¼ teaspoon ground cumin
3 tablespoons extra virgin olive oil

Serves 4

Peter Doyle, Celsius
Dukkah

Dukkah is a spice mix which tastes good with beer—place a small amount in a shallow bowl next to some olive oil in a small dish and serve with crusty bread. Dip the end of the bread into the oil and then into the dukkah. Yum.

1 To make the dukkah, roast the sesame seeds on a small baking tray in a preheated oven at 175°C for 8 minutes, until aromatic. At the same time, roast the coriander seeds for 4 minutes on a separate tray and the almond meal for 5 minutes on another tray.
2 Remove from the oven as they are ready and place them in a large bowl. Add the cumin, salt and pepper and mix well. Blend the ingredients together in a food processor until they are finely crushed, but not as fine as a powder. Don't overprocess or the oil from the sesame seeds and almond will turn it into a paste instead of a crushed dry mixture. Store in an airtight jar—it will keep for 3–4 weeks.

1½ cups sesame seeds
1½ cups coriander seeds
½ cup white almond meal
½ cup ground cumin
1 teaspoon sea salt
½ teaspoon freshly ground black pepper

Serves 12

Barbara Beckett, food writer

Onion soup with lager

I am sure I'm not the only one who makes this well-known soup this way—it provides hearty flavours that make it worth imbibing at any time of the day. Make it with your favourite lager—the better the beer, the better the soup.

35 g unsalted butter
3–4 onions, thinly sliced
4 teaspoons flour
1½ cups favourite lager, heated
2½ cups beef stock or water, heated
8 thin slices of baguette
155 g Gruyère cheese
Salt and freshly ground black pepper

Serves 4

1 Melt the butter in a frying pan. Add the onions and cook over a low heat until they are golden, about 30 minutes. Sprinkle with the flour and stir it in. Add the lager and the stock or water and boil for 1 minute, stirring constantly.

2 Meanwhile, dry the bread in a preheated oven at 180°C and slice the cheese very thinly. Alternate layers of bread and cheese in a heat-proof soup tureen or a deep casserole pot. Pour the hot soup over the bread and cheese, season and brown in the hot oven for 30 minutes.

David Sampson, Lynwood Stores
Beer chutney

1 Place all the ingredients except the cornflour in a heavy-based saucepan and cook for 2½ hours over a medium heat. Mix the cornflour with a little water until smooth. Stir it into the chutney to amalgamate and cook for a further hour. Ladle into warm sterilised jars and seal when cool. Store in a dark, airy place. Perfect for a ploughman's lunch with cheddar and crusty bread.

1.5 kg carrots, cut into 5 mm dice
1 kg onions, cut into 5 mm dice
450 g celery, cut into 5 mm dice
8 cups stout
⅔ cup ground coriander
⅓ cup salt
⅓ cup freshly ground black pepper
1 tablespoon ground cloves
2 tablespoons ground allspice
1 tablespoon cayenne pepper
½ cup brown sugar
½ cup currants
¼ cup malt vinegar
⅔ cup tomato purée
⅓ cup mango chutney
⅓ cup finely grated fresh ginger
½ cup cornflour

18 serves

Barbara Beckett, food writer
Mussels cooked in white beer

Live mussels keep their shells tightly closed so discard any that are open.

1 Scrub the mussels clean in plenty of water and remove the beard with a sharp knife.
2 Place the butter, shallots and bouquet garni in a large saucepan and place the mussels, beer and pepper on top. Place over a high heat for 4–5 minutes or until the shells begin to open up. Remove the shells with tongs as they open. Discarding the empty half-shells, distribute the half-shells containing the mussels into 4 warm bowls. Discard any mussels that don't open. Ladle the cooking liquid and shallots into the bowls, garnish with coriander and serve.

2 kg mussels
40 g butter, diced
3 golden shallots, finely chopped
Bouquet garni of bay leaf, parsley and thyme
1½ cups white (wheat) beer
Freshly ground black pepper
2 tablespoons fresh chopped coriander

Serves 4

Tony Bilson

Foods that love beer

I was born with the smell of beer in my nostrils. My family owned and ran a pub in Liverpool, Western Sydney. We even used to bottle draught beer in a little bottling plant at the rear of the pub. The customers would bring their own bottles to be filled—some as large as jeroboams. So I think I can claim some sort of expertise with regard to beer. Yet beer, like cooking, has changed over the years, though the image of it as a beverage of good cheer remains.

It is only recently that artisanal brewing has become very popular. Although Coopers has been brewing for over 130 years, brewers like Geoff Scharer and Chuck Hahn are relative newcomers. I believe it is their efforts that have prompted the larger breweries to offer a greater range—many of which marry happily with food. At the same time, Australians have developed a wider appreciation of food and flavours that has mirrored the extended range of beers. And these foods combine well with beer.

To the expert beer lover, beer is as complex to study as wine. The flavours range from the rich, dark, fruity porters and stouts to the cleansing bitterness of hop-flavoured pilseners and white (wheat) beers. The range of foods enjoyed with beer varies according to the type of beer. Generally, as when matching food with wine, it is best to think in terms of the weight of the flavour of food when choosing a beer to accompany it. For instance, I prefer a light, white beer style with Thai curries because of their extreme heat and acidity. A darker ale marries well with Indian vindaloo curries.

The palest wheat beers are acidic so are wonderfully matched with that classic dish from Munich, veal sausages and sweet mustard. Pork sausages and a hot chutney make a fine alternative. Richer wheat beers, like Redback Original, team up with spicy veal dishes—perhaps a hot goulash sweetened with tomato.

My favourite beers fall in the mid-range of flavours. I seem to have a particular weakness for the flavour of Czechoslovakian hops. This aromatic plant gives beer a distinctive fruit aroma and marries particularly well with fish dishes.

The sweeter pilsener styles are best accompanied by grilled fish, steaming bowls of chowder and that old favourite, oyster soup. Try pilsener with cured fish such as gravlax or salt cod made into the classic dish from Provence, *brandade de morue*. Pilsener is suited to salty food, in particular, Portuguese fried chicken and grilled ribs of beef. The lighter lager styles are most suited to curries because their flavours refresh the palate after a spice assault.

Chicken sautéed with onions and Dijon mustard is another appetising dish in the same style. The classic trencherman's dish of tripes Lyonnaise is perfect to drink with a pint of dark lager.

For the darker lagers, I love to use strong mustards with beef and lamb—spread it over the meat before roasting or grilling. It forms a light, salty and savoury crust on the meat. Chicken sautéed with onions and Dijon mustard is another appetising dish in the same style. The classic trencherman's dish of tripes Lyonnaise is perfect to drink with a pint of dark lager.

Try roasting a chicken basted with ground cardamom, cumin, ginger and garlic mixed with a cup of melted butter. To achieve a nice crispy brown skin baste it constantly as it roasts. Finally, enjoy it with a fine pilsener. The darker lager or bock styles are beautifully teamed with those classic home-cooked dishes of braised beef—steak and kidney pie, or brisket slowly simmered in beer and served with a sauce piquant of mustard, cornichons and capers. Irresistible!

The darker ale styles like Toohey's Old are also excellent served with roast game. First marinate the meat with a mixture of vinegar, herbs and juniper berries and serve it with a reduction sauce made from the marinade and sweetened with red currant jelly. Delicious!

A good example of the way beer is used in European cooking is this German beer soup. Take ¼ cup of currants, 1 cup of fresh brown breadcrumbs, 2⅓ cups of beer, brown sugar and cream to taste. Swell the currants in a little warm water and drain. Add the breadcrumbs and beer. Allow to soak for a few hours then bring slowly to a simmer. Sprinkle with sugar and add cream to taste. This is a good hearty soup for winter and it illustrates the type of cooking normally associated with beer. As fine as it is though, it shouldn't necessarily set the pattern. I encourage cooks to be more adventurous and to use the many contrasting beer flavours now available in a more contemporary fashion.

My recipe for a stout sorbet results in an unusual flavour if you are used to fruit sorbets and ice creams, but this sorbet is perfect alone or teamed with the more neutral flavours of a bread and butter pudding. The fashionable habit of sucking lime with the lighter Mexican beers could just as easily inspire a sorbet based on a similar combination. Or perhaps a dish of lime-beer prawns, page 93.

Other interesting combinations? Well, my recipe for salmon on page 116 has a subtle flavour but is robust enough to be teamed with a really good pilsener to provide a wonderful harmony of flavours. I reiterate, be adventurous, there are many foods out there that love beer.

Tony Bilson's Stout sorbet, page 136, is equally good with a sweet biscuit or a bread and butter pudding. Accompanied, of course, by a little stout in a flute.

Peter Doyle, Celsius

Oyster beignets with gribiche sauce

Pacific oysters are cooked in a light beer batter and served with a piquant sauce of fresh herbs, hardboiled egg, capers and shallots. A perfect pairing of flavours to wash down with a cool lager on a summer's day.

Gribiche sauce

3 tablespoons hardboiled egg white
2 tablespoons hardboiled egg yolk
1½ tablespoons finely chopped golden shallots
3 teaspoons finely chopped capers
3 teaspoons finely chopped cornichons
1 teaspoon Dijon mustard
2 tablespoons sherry vinegar
½ cup extra virgin olive oil
½ teaspoon finely chopped fresh tarragon
2 teaspoons finely chopped fresh flat-leaf parsley
1 teaspoon finely chopped fresh chives

Beer batter

1 cup flour
5 tablespoons lager
3 tablespoons water
2 x 55 g eggs, separated

Vegetable oil for deep frying
24 Pacific oysters, Franklin Harbour if available, shucked
3 tablespoons flour for dusting
300 g rock salt for serving
Lemon wedges to garnish
Parsley leaves to garnish, optional

Serves 6

1 To make the gribiche sauce, place all the ingredients in a mixing bowl and stir together. The sauce can be prepared a few days in advance without the herbs which should be added just before serving. Keep covered, in the refrigerator.

2 To make the batter, mix the flour, lager, water and egg yolks together in a bowl to form a smooth mixture. Cover and set aside for 20 minutes. Just before using the batter, whisk the egg whites to stiff peaks and gently fold into the batter with a rubber spatula.

3 To cook the beignets, pour the oil into a deep saucepan until one-third full, and bring to the boil over a medium heat. Test to see if it is hot enough (180°C), by dropping a bread cube in. If it turns golden brown in less than 1 minute it is ready.

4 Remove the oysters from their shells and place them on kitchen paper to dry a little. Dust the oysters in a light coating of flour and shake off any excess. With tongs, dip eight of the oysters into the batter to coat them evenly and cook in the hot oil until crisp and lightly golden. Remove with a slotted spoon and drain on absorbent paper while you cook the remaining oysters.

5 Meanwhile, spoon about 1 tablespoon of the completed gribiche sauce into the cleanly washed oyster shells. Spread rock salt over half of each serving plate and arrange the shells in the salt—the salt holds the shells firm. Serve 3–4 oysters per serve. When the beignets are ready, add one to each shell, top with a parsley leaf if liked, and garnish each plate with lemon wedges.

Louise Harper, Oh! Calcutta

Machi pakorhas (fish fritters)

Crisp, spicy, light and delicious. Perfect to accompany a light beer!

Yoghurt chilli sauce

1 tablespoon ghee

2 teaspoons minced onion

¼ teaspoon minced garlic

¼ teaspoon minced ginger

¼ teaspoon ground coriander

¼ teaspoon chilli powder

Pinch turmeric

2 tablespoons yoghurt

⅓ cup cream

1 tablespoon lemon juice

1 tablespoon water

Machi pakorhas

½ cup chick pea flour

½ cup ground rice

¼ teaspoon baking powder

¾ teaspoon salt

1 teaspoon cumin seeds

1 teaspoon kolinji seeds or black mustard seeds

½ teaspoon garam masala

1 teaspoon chilli powder

¼ cup robust ale

⅔ cup cold water

20 curry leaves, sliced finely (fresh if available)

125 g whitebait

½ cup raw sweet potato, grated coarsely

2 spring onions, sliced thickly into 5 cm lengths

Vegetable oil for deep frying

Serves 6 as an appetiser

1 To make the yoghurt chilli sauce, heat the ghee in a frying pan over a medium heat. Gently fry the onion, garlic, ginger and spices until the onions are soft. Stir in the yoghurt and cream and mix until smooth. Add the lemon juice and water then set aside to cool.

2 To make the machi pakorhas, sieve the chick pea flour, ground rice, baking powder and salt into a large bowl. Stir in the cumin seeds, kolinji seeds, garam masala and chilli powder with a wooden spoon. Add the ale and cold water, gradually mixing to a thick batter. Add the curry leaves, whitebait, sweet potato and spring onions to the batter and mix thoroughly.

3 Fill a saucepan one-third deep with oil. Bring the oil to boil over a medium heat. When a piece of the batter goes golden within 1 minute, the oil is the correct temperature. Drop tablespoonsful of the mixture in batches into the oil and fry until golden on both sides. Lift out with a slotted spoon and drain on absorbent paper. Be careful not to overcrowd the saucepan. Serve the machi pakorhas with the yoghurt chilli sauce.

7. Hot days, cool flavours: summer mains

Liam Tomlin, Banc

Terrine of smoked salmon with crab salad

The saltiness of the anchovies and the smoked salmon are a perfect match for a cool lager. Serve as a light lunch.

Terrine

175 g unsalted butter, at room temperature

50 g marinated anchovies

Finely grated zest 1 lemon

Juice ½ lemon

2 tablespoons chopped fresh flat-leaf parsley

1 tablespoon sliced fresh chives

3 golden shallots, finely chopped

Salt and freshly ground black pepper

1–1.5 kg smoked salmon, finely sliced

Crab salad

240 g picked crab meat

12 golden shallots, sliced

3 tomatoes, peeled, seeded and diced

Fresh baby coriander leaves

Salt and freshly ground black pepper

Lemon juice

Lemon-flavoured olive oil or cold-pressed virgin olive oil

Serves 12

1 To make the terrine, line a 1.4 kg terrine mould or a 900 g loaf tin with cling wrap leaving a 2 cm overhang on each side. Place the butter in a bowl. Cut the anchovies into small dice and mash into the butter. Add the lemon zest, juice, parsley, chives and golden shallots. Season to taste with salt and pepper.

2 Cover the base of the lined terrine with a layer of the smoked salmon, ensuring there are no holes or gaps. Using a palette knife, spread a thin layer of the butter over the smoked salmon covering the entire surface. Continue to build the terrine with alternating layers of smoked salmon and butter until all the ingredients are used up or the terrine is full, making the last layer smoked salmon. Cover the top of the terrine with cling wrap and place a 1 kg weight on top. Transfer to the refrigerator and leave overnight to allow the butter to set.

3 To make the crab salad, mix the crab meat, golden shallots, tomato dice and coriander together gently in a bowl. Season with salt, pepper and lemon juice. Bind with a little of the lemon oil.

4 To serve, turn the set terrine out by using a very sharp knife to cut through the cling wrap. This will help keep the shape of the terrine. Remove the cling wrap and brush the sides of the terrine with a little lemon oil to give it a nice shine. Place the terrine on a plate and allow it to stand at room temperature for 15 minutes to soften the butter. Spoon a small pile of crab salad at either end of the terrine and drizzle a little more oil around the plate.

PREVIOUS PAGE: *Stefano Manfredi's Roast red emperor with braised zucchini and a bread and tarragon salsa. For recipe see page 97.*

Philip Johnson, e'cco

Salad of cuttlefish, pawpaw, chilli, lime and cashews

A perfect salad to partner a rich malty pilsener that has a hint of sweetness balanced by bitterness. The fragrant and versatile Thai-style dressing can be used with both seafood and meat salads. From my new book, e'cco 2.

600 g medium cuttlefish
2 tablespoons light olive oil or peanut oil

Lime and palm sugar dressing

1 cup fresh lime juice
1½ cups palm sugar
1 chilli, roughly chopped
Few fresh coriander roots, washed
Few fresh basil and mint stems, washed
2 Kaffir lime leaves
2 tablespoons roughly chopped fresh ginger
1 stalk fresh lemongrass, soft part only, bruised
Good dash fish sauce to taste

Salad

2–3 Continental cucumbers, peeled, cut into fine strips
1 small green pawpaw, skin and seeds removed, sliced into fine julienne
2 spring onions, finely sliced diagonally
1–2 red chillies, sliced into fine julienne
1 cup fresh coriander sprigs, washed and picked over
¼ cup fresh mint leaves, washed
¼ cup toasted unsalted cashews

½ cup Asian fried onions
3 limes, halved

Serves 6

1 If possible, buy the cuttlefish already cleaned and simply score it. Otherwise, prepare the cuttlefish by slicing it lengthwise through the body. Open up the body and remove the insides including the cuttle bone. Pull the skin away from the flesh and discard along with the tentacles. Wash and dry the flesh. Using a very sharp knife, score the flesh into a diamond pattern, being careful not to cut right through. Put the cuttlefish with the olive oil in a bowl, cover and refrigerate until required.

2 To make the lime and palm sugar dressing, bring the lime juice to the boil in a saucepan over a medium heat. Remove from the heat, add the palm sugar and stir until it dissolves, returning to the heat if necessary. In a mortar and pestle lightly crush the chilli, herbs, lime leaves, ginger and lemongrass. Add this to the lime juice and palm sugar. Allow to infuse for 1 hour. Set aside to cool, seasoning to taste with the fish sauce. Strain before using.

3 To make the salad, combine all the ingredients in a bowl and add enough dressing to moisten them.

4 To cook the cuttlefish, drain off excess oil and season with salt and pepper. Heat a heavy-based frying pan or barbecue plate over a high heat. Place the cuttlefish, score-side down, in the hot pan and cook until a good colour is achieved, turning once; 1–2 minutes on each side should be enough.

5 To serve, place 2–3 pieces of cuttlefish in the centre of each plate, arrange the salad on top and then top this with a final piece of cuttlefish. Drizzle extra dressing over the cuttlefish and salad. Sprinkle with the fried onions and serve with lime halves.

Maggie Beer, food writer

Flathead in beer batter

When I first tasted my late mother-in-law's beer batter I was astounded by its lightness—she prepared it 24 hours in advance. Recipe from Maggie's Table.

1 To make the batter, whisk the ingredients in a bowl until smooth. Cover with cling film and refrigerate for 24 hours.
2 Pour the olive oil into a shallow heavy-based frying pan, leaving enough room to add the fish without spilling the oil. Heat the oil over a medium heat until hot enough that a bread cube when dropped in turns golden within 1 minute. Dip the flathead fillets into the beer batter to coat, then gently lower them into the hot oil—you will need to do this in batches. Fry until crisp and golden brown on one side then turn to cook the other. Transfer to slices of stale bread to drain. Serve with salt, pepper and lemon.

Beer batter
2 cups self-raising flour
½ cup light lager
1 cup cold water

Extra virgin olive oil
6 flathead fillets, skin removed
Slices stale bread, optional
Sea salt and freshly ground black pepper
10 lemon wedges

Serves 6

Tony Bilson, chef and food writer

Prawns sautéed with beer and lime

Inspired by the fashionable habit of sucking lime with light Mexican beer.

1 To devein the prawns, remove the heads and shells. Slit along the back of the prawn with a sharp-pointed knife. Pull out and discard the intestinal vein and wash thoroughly in plenty of water.
2 Season the prawns with salt and pepper. Heat the oil in a frying pan over a medium heat. Add the prawns and the onion and cook until lightly coloured. Quickly add the zest and the beer, reduce the liquid until syrupy over a high heat. Add the chilli, lime juice and the chopped chervil, toss through the prawns and serve.

300 g prawns
Salt and freshly ground black pepper
2 tablespoons olive oil
2 tablespoons chopped onion
Pinch chopped lime zest
⅔ cup light lager
½ teaspoon chopped fresh chilli to taste
3 tablespoons lime juice
1 tablespoon chopped fresh chervil

Serves 2

Carol Selva Rajah, food writer
Chili ketam (Chilli crab)

Serve the crabs piping hot with a strongly hopped pilsener to balance the spices.

2 x 1 kg mud crabs
2 tablespoons salted black soy beans
2 tablespoons oil
4 garlic cloves, roughly chopped
1 tablespoon ginger, pounded to make a paste
3 tablespoons sambal oelek
2 tablespoons sweet dark Chinese vinegar
½ cup white wine or Shao Hsing wine
1 tablespoon hoisin sauce or to taste
1 tablespoon tomato sauce
1 teaspoon sugar to blend flavours
Salt to taste
1 bunch spring onion, finely sliced diagonally

Serves 4

1 Cut the crabs in two and clean well. Crack the claws to allow the sauce to penetrate. Wash the soy beans and crush roughly.

2 Heat the oil in a large wok or stock pot over a medium heat. Brown the garlic and ginger until aromatic then add the sambal oelek and black soy beans. Stir well. Add the crabs and stir briskly then pour in the Chinese vinegar and wine. Cover the wok to steam the crab in the liquid. When the crab shells are red and the meat cooked, about 15 minutes, add the hoisin sauce, tomato sauce, sugar and salt to taste. Garnish with the spring onions and remove from the heat. Serve with bowls of steamed rice.

Carol Selva Rajah, food writer

Malaysian ikan sumbat (stuffed fish)

This is a wonderful dish to make with yellowtail or small snapper. These small fish make ideal individual servings on a bed of rice. Wash it down with a dry, light lager which has a fruity nose and a soft, malty palate.

1 To make the stuffing, dry roast the dessicated coconut and prawn powder in a dry frying pan over a medium heat until golden brown. Place all the stuffing ingredients in a blender or food processor and blend well. You may have to add extra coconut milk or water to help when grinding. Place the oil in a frying pan over a low heat and when hot, add the stuffing. Slow roast for 10 minutes until it is aromatic and some of the raw taste is eliminated. Remove from the heat and reserve.

2 To stuff the fish, insert a knife into the stomach cavity of the fish between the bone and skin without breaking the skin. Make a slit under the bone to make space for the filling. Fill the cavity and stomach with the cooked stuffing. Mix together the turmeric, salt and oil and brush over each fish.

3 The fish may be grilled under a preheated hot griller for 10–15 minutes on each side. Alternatively, try grilling the fish on a banana leaf placed on a barbecue grill—the fish remains clean and unbroken. It may also be shallow-fried in hot oil—skewer the fish with a bamboo skewer through the cavity. This makes them easy to turn and looks attractive, while retaining the filling in the cavity.

Stuffing

- ½ cup dessicated coconut
- 1 tablespoon dry prawn powder (available at Asian shops)
- ½ teaspoon salt
- 1 red onion, finely sliced
- 3 garlic cloves, chopped
- 2 teaspoons fresh ginger, chopped or pounded
- 2 stalks fresh lemongrass, soft part only, chopped
- 1 tablespoon sambal oelek or chilli flakes
- 1 teaspoon tamarind paste or purée
- ¼ cup fresh Vietnamese or common variety mint leaves, chopped
- About ½ cup coconut milk

- 1 tablespoon oil
- 4 x 150 g small snapper or yellowtail, cleaned and gutted
- ½ teaspoon turmeric
- ½ teaspoon salt
- 1 teaspoon oil

Serves 4

Beer makes you feel as you ought to feel without beer.
HENRY LAWSON

Chris Taylor, Fraser's

Whitebait, parsley and pancetta fritters

This is a great accompaniment to a big-flavoured bitter lager with a pronounced hop character. The strong flavours of the pancetta and tamarind dipping sauce make these fritters a firm favourite. Serve at cocktail parties or as a starter.

Beer batter

1½ cups bitter lager
1¼ cups self-raising flour
1 cup plain flour
Dash vinegar

Tamarind dipping sauce

¾ cup sugar
5 tablespoons vinegar
1 chilli, deseeded
1 tablespoon finely chopped fresh ginger
2 garlic cloves, peeled
½ stick fresh lemongrass, soft part only
2 cardamom pods
2 cinnamon sticks
1 teaspoon ground cumin seeds
1 teaspoon ground coriander seeds
200 g tomatoes, skinned, deseeded and chopped
1 x 200 g packet tamarind, soaked in 1 cup warm water

Fritters

240 g whitebait
20 sprigs fresh flat-leaf parsley
⅔ cup beer batter
4 slices pancetta, roughly chopped
Vegetable oil for deep-frying
Sea salt
1 red chilli, deseeded and finely sliced
6 lemon wedges

Serves 6

1 To make the beer batter, mix the ingredients in a bowl to form a smooth batter. Cover and set aside to rest for 20 minutes. Whisk again just before using.

2 To make the tamarind dipping sauce, caramelise the sugar and vinegar over a medium heat and cook until the liquid begins to brown. Add the remaining ingredients except for the tomato and tamarind and cook for 5 minutes. Drain the seeds from the tamarind water and discard. Add the tomato and tamarind water to the sauce. Pass the sauce through a course strainer and adjust the seasoning.

3 To make the fritters, mix together the whitebait, parsley, beer batter and pancetta in a large bowl. Heat a frying pan or wok over a high heat and pour in the oil. Heat until a slight heat haze starts to rise from the oil. Using 2 tablespoons, place about 24 spoonfuls of whitebait mixture into the oil—this may have to be done in batches so as not to crowd the pan. When the fritters are golden brown, after about 2 minutes, remove and place on absorbent paper to drain. Place in a bowl and season with the sea salt and chopped chilli. Serve on a cloth or paper with the tamarind dipping sauce and lemon wedges.

'If the beer has big flavours match it with strong-flavoured food. It is important to use the right beer when cooking, that is, to respect the qualities of the beer.'

Chris Taylor, Fraser's

Stefano Manfredi, bel mondo

Roast red emperor with braised zucchini and a bread and tarragon salsa

The richly textured, large-flaked red emperor is ideal for roasting as it can be cut as a thick piece. A medium-bodied premium lager is perfect to drink with the clean complex flavours of the tarragon-and-bread salsa accompaniment.

1 To make the salsa, put the bread in a bowl and moisten with the vinegar until it is completely absorbed. Place the bread, tarragon and the garlic into a food processor and turn the motor on while pouring the olive oil in slowly. Continue until it is well blended. Season to taste and store in a clean jar in the refrigerator until needed. It will last about a week.

2 To cook the zucchini, heat the olive oil in a large frying pan over a high heat. Add the zucchini, onions and garlic. Stir constantly with a wooden spoon so that it doesn't stick to the pan. Do this until the onions have softened, about 2–3 minutes. Add the tomatoes and simmer until the zucchini are cooked but not too soft, about 8–10 minutes. Turn off the heat, mix in the parsley and season to taste with salt and pepper. Cover and keep warm.

3 To cook the fish, place the oil in a frying pan over a high heat. Sear the fish on both sides for 30 seconds each and then finish the cooking in a preheated oven at 200°C for 4–5 minutes. Serve the fish on the salsa with the zucchini scattered around the warm plates.

Bread and tarragon salsa

- 2 slices day-old white bread, crusts removed
- 6 tablespoons red wine vinegar
- 1 cup fresh tarragon leaves
- 1 garlic clove, minced
- ¼ cup extra virgin olive oil
- Salt and freshly ground black pepper

Braised zucchini

- ¼ cup extra virgin olive oil
- 500 g zucchini, cut 2 cm wide x 5 cm long
- 2 medium onions, sliced top to bottom, about 5 mm thick
- 3 garlic cloves, minced
- 150 g tomatoes, roughly chopped
- ⅓ cup roughly chopped fresh flat-leaf parsley
- Salt and freshly ground black pepper

- 2 tablespoons extra virgin olive oil
- 8 x 150 g red emperor pieces, skin on

Serves 8

Of doctors and medicines we have in plenty more than enough? What you may send, for the Love of God, is some large quantity of beer.

DISPATCH FROM THE COLONY OF
NEW SOUTH WALES, 1854.

Kate Sparrow, Petaluma's Bridgewater Mill

Chicken and squid salad

I have become addicted to the fresh and exhilarating flavours of Vietnamese food by my partner Le Tu Thai and his mother. This salad is a combination of cooked, raw and pickled food with a rich variety of textures and flavours.

Nuôc mám dressing

2 garlic cloves, peeled and finely chopped

2 medium-size mild fresh chillies, finely chopped

Juice 1 lime

5 tablespoons coconut vinegar

⅔ cup fish sauce

5 tablespoons sugar

Pickled mango and carrot

⅔ cup white vinegar

3 tablespoons sugar

1 teaspoon salt

1¼ cups water

1 small carrot, peeled and julienne

1 green mango, peeled and julienne

2 medium-size whole fresh squid

Salad

1 Lebanese cucumber, seeded and julienne

1 lemon grass stalk, tender part, finely chopped

1 tablespoon shredded fresh coriander leaves

Garnish

24 fresh mint leaves

1 tablespoon fried Asian shallots (available from Chinese grocers)

2 tablespoons roasted peanuts, roughly chopped

Chicken

1 large breast free-range chicken

1 tablespoon peanut oil

Salt

Serves 6

1 To make the nuôc mám dressing, place all the ingredients into a bowl and mix together, adjusting the chilli if necessary. The dressing may be made several days in advance and kept refrigerated until needed. Use it also for grilled seafood, pork, poultry and beef.

2 To make the pickles, place the vinegar, sugar, salt and water in a saucepan and bring to the boil over a medium heat. Stir occasionally to dissolve the sugar. Remove from the heat and let cool. Place the carrot and mango in a bowl with the cold pickling liquid. Mix well, cover with cling film and refrigerate until ready to use. It may be made several days in advance.

3 To prepare the squid, gently pull the head with its tentacles from the body. Discard the head and cut the tentacles into 4 pieces and reserve. Peel the membrane from the squid tube and cut along the length of the tube. Open it out and remove the transparent quill and any remaining guts. Rinse thoroughly in plenty of cold water.

4 Flatten out the clean squid tubes on your chopping board with the inside facing you. With a sharp knife score ⅔ deep into the flesh diagonally and repeat again to make a diamond pattern. Be careful not to cut through the flesh. Cut into cross sections about 2 cm long.

5 To cook the squid, place a large pot of salted water on the stove and bring to the boil over a medium heat. The secret of tender squid is not to overcook it. Place the prepared squid, including the tentacles, in the boiling water and cook for about 30 seconds or until the squid has curled up. Remove with a slotted spoon and set aside.

Recipe continues on page 102

Len Evans
A wine lover's guide to beer

Once upon a time, beer and wine were drunk from the same type of glass. Old or new, a good quality glass enhances our enjoyment.

TALK about Daniel in the lion's den.

Beer? I didn't drink the stuff for years, even when I worked as a labourer in Mount Isa.

But let me explain! In 1955 consumption of table wine in Australia was about one glass per head per year. In 1965, I was asked to take over promotion for the Australian wine industry, consumption by then being about one bottle per head per year. Beer was the enemy, because beer was king. Beer consumption wasn't mentioned in glasses or bottles but in gallons. During that time the Northern Territorians were the greatest consumers of beer in the world.

When I was a glass-washer at the Ship Inn at Circular Quay in the late 1950s, the 'six o'clock swill' was in full swing. Workers would rush in at 5.30 and order six schooners—all for themselves, for they lined them up on the bar or a ledge and stood and drank them one after the other.

But beer wasn't just the workers' drink. Posters of the day extolling the sociability of beer portrayed sleek men in white tie and tails and women in glamorous, full-length gowns, seated in night clubs, listening to the music, or dancing—when dancing was still a contact sport. And what was on the tables or in the ice buckets? Bottles of beer.

When in 1960 I became beverage manager of Australia's brightest, newest—and probably first international-standard—hotel, beer still appeared on more tables than wine, though this changed during the time I was there. We sold lots of beer in the hotel bars, but there was more profit in wine. But, wine or beer, it was all fun.

I'm a gregarious fellow, I can sit at a dinner table for hours drinking all sorts of wines. Yet I must confess I can't stand at a bar with my friends drinking beer after beer, even of different styles. Quite simply, for me it does not have the same appeal. All of which, therefore, would indicate I'm not a lover of good beer—but nothing could be farther from the truth. So there's the paradox!

In fact, I greatly enjoy good beer. I like my beer to be like wine, to have a good fruity nose, fine bead, delicacy and intensity of flavour on the tongue, length and finesse. These days such qualities are almost as easy to find in Australia as they are in Europe, particularly among the small-brewery, boutique beers. When our beer is good, it is very good indeed.

Years ago I played golf with a chap on a very hot day. As we finished the round and headed for the clubhouse he said, 'My God, I've got a thirst I wouldn't sell for a thousand bucks.'

That's the real point. Nothing quenches a real thirst in the same way that a good beer does. What is so special is the taste, particularly the first taste, of a fine beer. There is nothing like the first sip of a really cold, top-quality beer as it hits the mouth, cleans the palate, refreshes the tongue and slides like a liquid avalanche down the throat—there's really nothing like it at all.

Good beer, dry, softly effervescing and redolent of hops, can be like a good wine. On a really hot day, it can refresh, titillate, and satisfy, as it seems to evaporate in the mouth and throat.

Just the thought of that first taste makes me thirsty.

A matchless sight at day's end.

Chicken and squid salad continued from page 98

6 Prepare the salad and garnish ingredients ready for compiling the final dish.

7 To cook the chicken, brush it with peanut oil, season with salt and place under a preheated hot grill. When golden brown, turn and sear again until cooked through and the juices run clear when pierced with a fine skewer. Remove from the heat and rest at room temperature until ready to use.

8 To assemble the salad, drain the pickled mango and carrot in a sieve. In a large bowl, mix the mango and carrot with the prepared salad of cucumber, lemongrass and coriander. Slice the chicken into bite-size pieces. Divide the salad into 4 and arrange on the serving plates with the squid and sliced chicken. Spoon over the dressing and garnish with the mint leaves, fried shallots and peanuts.

David Sampson, Lynwood Stores

Chicken à la bière

This chicken has a smooth, velvety sauce with a subtle flavour of beer. Serve with creamed potatoes and a glass or two of stout.

1.5 kg chicken thighs or breasts

2 tablespoons butter or olive oil + extra

12 golden shallots, roughly chopped

Plain flour for dusting

1 cup stout

2 cups chicken stock

3 rashers bacon

250 g button mushrooms

1 sprig fresh lemon thyme

1 sprig fresh rosemary

1 fresh bay leaf

2 pinches of salt

2 pinches freshly ground black pepper

Pinch cayenne

½ cup cream

2 tablespoons freshly chopped flat-leaf parsley to garnish

Serves 5

1 Dust the chicken with a little flour. Place the fat in a frying pan over a medium heat and when hot sauté the chicken until it begins to colour. Remove from the pan. Sauté the shallots until golden brown. Place the chicken and shallots in an earthenware casserole and pour over the stout and chicken stock.

2 Cut the bacon into small pieces 5 mm x 5 mm x 30 mm long. Wash the mushrooms and sauté for a few minutes in the pan in extra fat if necessary. Sauté the bacon until brown. Add the bacon and mushrooms to the chicken along with the herbs, salt, pepper and cayenne. Place a tight-fitting lid on top. Put into a preheated oven at 170°C for about 1½ hours.

3 Place the cream in a saucepan and reduce by half over a high heat. Take the chicken out of the casserole and keep warm. Pour the sauce into the cream and reduce the sauce by ¼ over a high heat. Remove the herbs. Serve the chicken on a warm platter covered with sauce and parsley.

Alain Fabrègues, The Loose Box
Cloistered rabbit Bohemian

By using a spicy pale lager such as pilsener, the delicate rabbit flavours are not overpowered while the crisp, hoppy character of the beer is retained in the sauce.

1 fresh, farmed rabbit, about 1.2 kg
1 carrot
1 onion
2 garlic cloves
3 bottles (325 ml each) pilsener
1 bunch silver beet
2 litres cold water + 1 cup extra
1 teaspoon salt
Juice 1 lemon
4 tablespoons plain flour
2 tablespoons cornflour
2 tablespoons butter + extra
5 cups virgin olive oil
Salt and freshly ground black pepper
1 tablespoon Dijon mustard
⅘ cup chicken stock
⅘ cup cream
Leaves from 8 celery stalks, cleaned and dried
Vegetable oil for deep-frying

Serves 4

1 Marinate the rabbit for about 12 hours or overnight. Cut it into 8 pieces and place in a large bowl. Dice the carrot and onion and add to the rabbit. Leaving the skins on, mash the garlic cloves and place in the dish. Pour the pilsener over the ingredients and cover with cling film. Place in the refrigerator to marinate, turning every few hours.

2 The next day, wash the silver beet and remove the green leaves from the stalks and discard. Trim the stalks then cut them into 6 cm lengths. Bring the water to the boil in a large saucepan over a medium heat. Add the salt and lemon juice. In a small bowl combine the flour with the extra 1 cup water then add to the boiling water to make a blanc. (Blanc is a French term for a mixture of water and flour used for cooking white meats and some vegetables.) Add the silver beet stems, cover and cook for 45 minutes over a low heat. Remove from the heat and reserve the silver beet in the blanc until needed.

3 Remove the rabbit pieces from the marinade but reserve the beer and vegetable marinade for the sauce. Pat the rabbit dry with absorbent paper and toss the meat in the cornflour. Heat the butter and oil in a large frying pan over a medium heat and sauté the rabbit pieces until golden brown on all sides. Remove the rabbit and, using the same pan, brown the drained vegetables from the marinade. Season to taste. Remove any excess oil from the pan then add the beer from the marinade. Simmer until reduced to ⅓ of its volume or until the juices thicken. Stir the mustard into the juices then add the chicken stock and reduce again to ⅓ its volume. Add the cream, stirring until the sauce thickens, then pour through a sieve into a clean saucepan. Place over a low heat and when it is simmering, add the rabbit pieces and simmer a further 8 minutes. Remove from the heat but keep covered and warm.

4 To make the celery garnish, plunge the dry celery leaves into simmering hot oil. (The oil is hot enough when it turns a bread cube golden in 1 minute.) Cool the leaves for 1 minute on absorbent paper then sprinkle with a pinch of salt. Keep them warm until required.

5 To assemble the dish, remove the silver beet stalks from the blanc and toss them in a little melted butter. Add a pinch of salt and pepper. Distribute the silver beet on 4 warm plates. Put two rabbit pieces beside the silver beet. If you have a little hand blender, froth the sauce before pouring it over the rabbit. Place the celery leaves on top and serve.

Margaret Fulton, *New Idea*

Spiced grilled chicken

For those who enjoy variety and spice here's the very thing, chicken—young spatchcocks (poussins) or chicken pieces in a devilish sauce. Serve hot from the grill or barbecue with your favourite icy cold beer. Or take cold to a picnic.

1 Wipe the chicken dry with absorbent paper. If using whole chickens, split in half, cut away the back and rib bones.

2 Combine the ingredients for the spice in a bowl and mix well. Using a small palette knife spread the mixture over the chicken skin, and in between the skin and the loose flesh of the birds.

3 Preheat the grill to high. Line the grill pan with aluminium foil. Brush the grill rack with oil. Grill the chicken skin side up for 10 minutes, about 10 cm from the source of heat. Reduce the heat, turn and brush with the drippings and cook for a further 15 minutes. Turn the chicken again and cook a further 5 minutes or until cooked through. The juices run clear when pierced in the thickest part of the flesh with a fine skewer. Leave to rest a few minutes before serving.

4 To serve warm, arrange the salad greens on a platter and top with the chicken (chicken halves may be cut in two). Place the lemon wedges around decoratively. The warm chicken fatigues the salad greens; drippings from the grill pan may be drizzled over the chicken. Or serve cold, with thin Middle Eastern bread as a wrap.

4 x 500 g spatchcocks (poussins) or 8 chicken pieces, breasts or legs

Spice mix

2 tablespoons ground coriander

1 teaspoon ground cumin

½ teaspoon ground Mexican chilli powder or Moroccan harissa

1 garlic clove, crushed

1 lime, grated rind and juice

Sea salt and freshly ground black pepper

2 tablespoons vegetable or olive oil + extra

Salad greens for 8

Lemon wedges

Crusty bread or flat Middle Eastern bread

Serves 8

Lyndey Milan, *The Australian Women's Weekly*

Lamb with Thai mint dressing

The higher malt levels of a premium lager match the richness of the lamb.

About 1 kg easy-carve lamb leg roast
Salt and freshly ground black pepper
Thai mint dressing
4 large sprigs fresh mint
2 red chillies, seeds removed
12 golden shallot segments or 4 spring onions
3 cloves garlic
120 g cup palm sugar or brown sugar
⅔ cup fresh lime juice
2 tablespoons Thai fish sauce
Rice salad
1½ cups jasmine rice
2 carrots, peeled and diced
2 sticks celery, finely sliced
Serves 6

1 Preheat the oven to 200°C. Rub the lamb with black pepper and rub salt on the fat only. Place in a baking dish and bake for 40 minutes for medium rare, or longer if preferred. Rest in a warm place for 10 minutes.

2 Meanwhile, prepare the dressing, chop the mint, chillies, shallots and garlic in a food processor. Blend in the remaining dressing ingredients and reserve.

3 To cook the rice, bring 2 litres of salted water to the boil. Add the rice and 5 minutes later, the carrots. Cook until tender, around 17–20 minutes. Pour into a colander to drain and immediately place under a running cold tap until the rice is cold. Shake well to remove excess moisture. Stir the celery through and flavour with salt and pepper to taste.

4 To serve, carve the lamb. Place a mound of rice on each plate, top with some lamb and spoon the dressing over.

Louise Harper, Oh! Calcutta

Kangaroo sahk dhada

500 g kangaroo fillet or camel rump
2 teaspoons crushed garlic
½ teaspoon white pepper
1½ teaspoons cumin seeds, coarsely ground
½ teaspoon ground coriander
¼ teaspoon chilli powder
1 teaspoon salt
2 tablespoons white vinegar
3 teaspoons ghee
Good squeeze of lemon juice
1 tablespoon chopped fresh coriander leaves
1 teaspoon toasted sesame seeds
Serves 4

1 Cut the kangaroo or camel into 2 cm cubes and rub with the garlic, white pepper, cumin, coriander, chilli powder, salt and vinegar. Marinate it overnight covered in cling film.

2 Heat a wok or frying pan over a high heat and then heat the ghee. When the ghee is very hot, add the kangaroo or camel and stir-fry until the meat is tender, about three minutes.

3 Remove from the heat and stir in the lemon juice, chopped coriander leaves and toasted sesame seeds.

'I discovered the original recipe for camel years ago when travelling through Afghanistan. I find kangaroo fillet makes an excellent substitute.'

Sue Fairlie-Cuninghame, *Inside Out*

Truffle burgers

An extravagant but delicious dish. Serve it with a refreshing India pale ale.

1 In a small pan over a low heat melt 50 g of the butter and gently cook the garlic for 4–5 minutes making sure it does not colour. Place the garlic in a bowl and add the mince with salt and pepper to taste and half the truffle-infused oil. Mix very well with your hands, taste and add more truffle oil and seasoning if required. Put the mixture in the refrigerator, covered in cling film, for 2 hours.

2 Meanwhile, heat 75 g butter and a little olive oil over a low heat. Put in the onions, add the sugar, salt and pepper and some red wine vinegar to taste and cook until tender.

3 Heat the grill or an oiled ridged pan and grill the baguette slices. Keep them warm while you shape the burgers into 7 cm diameter x 3 cm thick patties. Rest the burgers for 5 minutes then grill under a preheated hot grill for 2 minutes on each side, turning once. Butter the baguette, top with a burger and a spoonful of onion.

150 g butter
2–3 cloves garlic, crushed
1 kg medium-ground premium beef mince
Sea salt and freshly ground black pepper
75 ml Terrabianca Truffle-infused Extra Virgin Olive Oil or similar
750 g red onions, peeled and sliced finely
Olive oil
1 teaspoon castor sugar
Red wine vinegar
1 fresh baguette, cut in diagonal slices 2 cm thick
Butter for serving

Makes about 12

Margaret Fulton, *New Idea*

Leg of ham baked in stout with spiced peaches

Serve the ham at room temperature with the spiced peaches and little pots of mustards, chutney and pickles. The long baking allows the wonderful flavour of the stout and cardamom, cloves and ginger to flavour the meat.

7–8 kg cured leg of ham

Stout glaze

3 cups stout

2 cups firmly packed brown sugar

2 tablepoons Dijon mustard

1 teaspoon ground ginger

2 teaspoons ground cardamom

Whole cloves

Watercress or parsley to garnish

Spiced peaches

3 x 825 g cans peach halves

½ teaspoon whole cloves

2.5 cm piece cinnamon stick

8 whole allspice

¼ cup brandy

½ cup sugar

¼ cup white vinegar

2 oranges, sliced

Extra cloves, optional

Serves 20–25

1 The skin must be removed before heating the ham up. Neatly cut away the skin with a boning knife from the thick end of the ham shank and ease the skin from the fat. Turn the ham over and ease away the rest of the skin which should come off in one piece. This is best done by sliding a clean hand between the ham and skin, removing the skin without tearing the fat. Discard the skin. You could ask the butcher to do this for you but make sure he leaves a good layer of fat on.

2 Line the baking tin with foil to make cleaning up easier. Place the ham, fat side uppermost, on a rack in the roasting tin and pour 2¾ cups of stout over. Cover the ham and tin with foil, making it as airtight as possible, and bake in a preheated oven at 160°C for 2½ hours, basting occasionally with stout. If the pan looks dry, add enough water so it won't burn.

3 Remove the ham from the oven and baste again. Score the fat with 5 mm deep diagonal cuts first one way, then the opposite way, to form a diamond pattern. Mix the sugar, mustard, ginger and cardamom together and add enough stout to moisten. Using a brush, spread the mixture over the ham. Stud every second diamond with a clove.

4 Increase the oven temperature to 200°C and bake the ham for a further 30–40 minutes. Serve at room temperature, garnished with watercress.

5 To make the spiced peaches, drain them and reserve 1 cup of the syrup. Put the syrup, cloves, cinnamon, allspice, brandy, sugar, vinegar and orange slices into a saucepan. Bring to the boil over a low heat, add the peaches and simmer for 5 minutes. Cover and allow to cool. Chill in the refrigerator. If liked, stud the fruit with extra cloves. Best made a week in advance and stored in the refrigerator.

8. Cold days, warm comfort: winter mains

Louise Harper, Oh! Calcutta

Jhinga kari (south Indian prawn curry)

This is a delicious, mild curry of butterflied prawns. You will definitely be back for more. It's perfect with a rich, malty, hoppy pilsener.

1 To butterfly the prawns, remove the shell and legs but retain the tail. Split them not quite through lengthwise and open them out like a butterfly. Remove the intestine then wash and dry the prawns thoroughly. Set aside.

2 Heat the ghee in a frying pan over a medium heat and when hot, fry the onion, garlic and ginger, stirring frequently, until the onions are soft. Add the turmeric, paprika and coriander and continue to fry for 1 minute. Add the prawns, stirring frequently until the prawns are half cooked, about 60 seconds. Mix in the coconut milk, water, tamarind and salt and stir well.

3 Meanwhile, mix the garnish ingredients in a bowl. The prawns are cooked in about another 2 minutes and the gravy will have slightly thickened. Serve sprinkled with the garnish and with a big glass of chilled pilsener.

250 g king prawns
4 tablespoons ghee
1 tablespoon brown onion, finely chopped
2 teaspoons minced garlic
2 teaspoons minced ginger
1 teaspoon turmeric
1 teaspoon paprika
2 teaspoons ground coriander
⅔ cup coconut milk
½ cup water
2 teaspoons tamarind pulp
½ teaspoon salt

Garnish

Cucumber, cut in half lengthwise, seeded and thinly sliced
Thinly sliced red onion
Red chilli slivers
Torn coriander leaves

Serves 2

Colonial beer banter

Brewery loafer Men who haunted breweries looking for free beer.
Good drop or not a bad drop A good beer.
Rabbit A bottle of beer.
Run the rabbit To fetch beer from a hotel.
She-oak A colonial word for beer, derived from a stand of she-oaks growing abundantly near Melbourne's first brewery which opened in 1837.
Shypoo joint or shypook A sly-grog shop.
Tanglefoot, squirt, stringy-bark, shearer's joy and jerrawicke All terms for colonial beer.

Previous page: David Pugh's Seafood and lemongrass broth. For recipe see page 112.

David Pugh, II (two)
Seafood and lemongrass broth

A fragrant, fresh seafood broth to drink with a nice light lager or pilsener.

2 stalks fresh lemongrass
12 fresh coriander leaves
5 cups chicken stock
2 teaspoons palm sugar
2 red chillies, deseeded and sliced
1 small knob fresh galangal, finely sliced
6 fresh Kaffir lime leaves
1 stalk fresh mint
1 tablespoon fish sauce
12 large green prawns, shelled and deveined
6 Moreton Bay bug tails, shells removed
125 g cuttlefish, trimmed and cut into strips
12 scallops
Juice 2 limes

Serves 6

1 To prepare the flavourings, remove the outside leaves of the lemongrass and discard. Finely slice the soft part on an angle. Divide it and the coriander between 6 bowls.
2 To prepare the broth, bring the stock, sugar, chillies, galangal, lime leaves, mint and fish sauce to the boil in a large saucepan over a medium heat. When it boils, turn down to a simmer then add the prawns and bug tails. Allow to simmer for 2 minutes. Add the cuttlefish strips and scallops and cook for a further 30 seconds. Remove the mint stalk and add the lime juice. Divide between the 6 bowls and serve immediately.

Joan Campbell, *Vogue Entertaining and Travel*
Prawns cooked in beer

Eat these delectable prawns with a winter salad of asparagus, beans and fennel and some warm Turkish bread. Serve with a glass of your favourite ale or lager.

1 kg green prawns
3½ cups bitter ale
2–3 cloves garlic, peeled and crushed
2 teaspoons salt
1 teaspoon chopped fresh thyme
3 bay leaves
1 teaspoon celery seeds
¼ teaspoon cayenne pepper
Juice 1 lemon

Serves 4 as a main, 6 as a starter

1 Devein the prawns, by removing the heads and shells only. Slit along the back of the prawn with a small sharp-pointed knife. Pull out and discard the intestinal vein. Wash thoroughly in plenty of water.
2 Put all of the ingredients except the prawns in a large saucepan and bring to the boil over a medium heat. Add the prawns and simmer for 3–5 minutes until the prawns are opaque. Test—the cooking time depends on size of prawns. Drain them and spread out on a cake rack to cool.
3 Serve the prawns at room temperature with a salad.

Cheong Liew, The Grange, Hilton Adelaide

Chilli and black bean mud crab braised with ale

Everyone likes to drink cold beer with Asian food but this recipe uses an amber ale as a braising liquid in the dish. It's sensational. The heat of the chilli and the saltiness of the black bean marries very well with the refreshing flavour of the ale.

1 Assemble and prepare all the ingredients. To kill the mud crab painlessly, use a pointed knife or a kitchen steel to pierce a hole between the crab's eyes. Scrub the crab thoroughly. Using a knife, cut under the top shell and remove the shell. Discard the innards and organs from the crab. Cut the crab into 4 sections. Crack the claws lightly with the flat of a chef's knife.

2 Season the crab with half the rice wine and the ginger juice. Dust each piece of crab with flour. Heat a wok or a large saucepan over a medium heat, then heat enough vegetable oil to deep-fry. When a bread cube goes golden within 1 minute it is ready. Deep-fry the crab until it is completely cooked, about 5 minutes, but check the largest claw for doneness. Remove and reserve.

3 In the cleaned wok or large frying pan heat the peanut oil over a medium heat and stir-fry the bamboo shoots, Chinese mushrooms, then garlic. Add the black beans, chilli and ginger and cook gently for 1 minute. Then add the scallops, water chestnut, spring onions and crab. Pour in the remaining rice wine and the soy. Stir-fry and pour in the ale. Cook over a high heat until the liquid is reduced by $\frac{1}{3}$, about 3 minutes. Add the oyster sauce and sugar and stir-fry. Garnish with fresh coriander and white pepper and serve immediately.

600 g live mud crab
2 tablespoons **Chinese rice wine**
1 tablespoon blended and strained fresh ginger juice
1 tablespoon wheat starch or cornflour, mixed with a little water
Vegetable oil for deep-frying
3 tablespoons peanut oil
6 pieces bamboo shoot
6 dried **Chinese mushrooms**, soaked for 15 minutes in hot water and drained
1 garlic clove, chopped
1 teaspoon **black beans**
2 dried chillies, finely chopped
6 slices fresh ginger
1 tablespoon soy sauce
6 scallops
10 water chestnuts
3 spring onions, cut into 4 cm batons
1½ cups amber ale
1 tablespoon oyster sauce
1 teaspoon sugar
3 sprigs fresh coriander
Freshly ground white pepper

Serves 2

Find me a bench, and let me snore,
Till, charged with ale and unconcern,
I'll think it's noon at half-past four!
                KENNETH SLESSOR

Damien Pignolet, Bistro Moncur

Lamb shoulder braised with parsley and ale

This dish is based on the taste of bitter ale, hence the parsley, thyme and leeks which provide herbaceous and earthy qualities with a slightly bitter finish. Particularly good to eat out-of-doors for a casual lunch in autumn or for a warming winter's dinner. Cook in an oven-to-table casserole accompanied by green beans or a salad. Enjoy a glass of ale with it.

2 lamb shoulders
200 g boneless, skinless pickled pork belly or 100 g bacon
2 large leeks
1 bunch parsley
½ bunch lemon thyme
500 g Kipfler or Pontiac potatoes
1 teaspoon salt
Freshly ground black pepper
150 g unsalted butter, melted
1¾ cups bitter ale

Serves 6

1 Remove the fat and skin from the lamb shoulders and dice the meat into 3 cm pieces. You need about 900 g. Cut the pickled pork or bacon into a fine dice. Wash the leeks and remove the green tops and root end. Slice the white part finely. Remove the leaves from the parsley and reserve, retaining 6 stalks. Bunch the parsley stalks with the lemon thyme and tie with kitchen string. Peel the potatoes and slice into 3 mm thick rounds.

2 In a large bowl mix the lamb, pork or bacon, leeks, parsley leaves and salt with plenty of pepper. Distribute the ingredients evenly then transfer to a direct-heat casserole leaving about 5 cm clearance at the top.

3 Push the bouquet into the middle of the dish. Cover with a layer of sliced potatoes, seasoning them with salt, pepper and melted butter. Make another layer overlapping neatly. Pour in the beer. Place the casserole over a medium heat and bring to the boil. Press the potatoes down with a spoon so they remain as a neat covering. Transfer to a preheated oven at 150°C, uncovered, for 2 hours or until the lamb is tender.

'Matching dishes to beverages requires the same palate considerations for beer as it does for wine. Qualities such as sweet, sour, acid and so on, need to be similar, or married with an opposite. The creamy palate of ale marries with the sweetness of lamb and the beer's bitterness is picked up by the large quantity of herbs used. Leeks and potatoes provide the fullness and follow-through on the palate.'
Damien Pignolet, Bistro Moncur

Tony Bilson, chef and food writer

Steamed cured salmon with cabbage

This elegant salmon dish is subtle in flavour but robust enough to be teamed with a really good pilsener, providing a wonderful marriage of flavours.

1.5 kg salmon, skin off, pin bones removed

Cure

⅓ cup white sugar

⅓ cup sea salt

4 sprigs fresh thyme

3 fresh bay leaves

1 tablespoon crushed fresh ginger

¼ teaspoon each ground star anise, ground coriander seeds, white pepper, ground cardamom seeds

Salmon stock

250 g salmon bones

5 tablespoons white wine

½ onion

½ carrot

½ stick celery

Sprig fresh thyme

1 bay leaf

1 teaspoon black peppercorns

Cabbage

50 g butter

1 finely sliced onion

2 garlic cloves, finely sliced

500 g savoy cabbage, finely shredded (use tender part only)

2½ tablespoons sherry vinegar

¾ cup salmon stock

Salt and freshly ground black pepper

1 tablespoon chopped, fresh flat-leaf parsley

Serves 6

1 To cure the salmon, mix all the curing ingredients together and rub over the salmon fillet. Place on a plate and cover with cling film. Leave to cure for 12 hours in the refrigerator. The next day, wipe the cure from the fillet with a damp cloth. Cut into 6 equal portions.

2 To make the salmon stock, place all the ingredients in a large saucepan with water to cover. Simmer over a low heat for 45 minutes. Strain through a sieve and when cold, remove the fat with a spoon and absorbent paper. Make the stock several hours in advance.

3 To cook the cabbage, soften the butter in a heavy frying pan over a low heat, add the onion and cook gently without browning the butter. Then add the garlic and continue to cook until softened. Add the cabbage and mix with the onion and garlic. Pour in the vinegar, stock, salt and pepper. Cook over a high heat to reduce the liquid until it coats the cabbage. Add the parsley just before serving. The cabbage will be tender and a fresh green colour.

4 To cook the salmon, steam it in a steamer over simmering water until it is cooked to the desired degree of doneness, about 7–10 minutes. The salmon is also very good if grilled. Feel free to choose your preferred method of cooking. Serve the salmon in the centre of warm plates with the cabbage on the side.

Liam Tomlin, Banc

Veal and bacon terrine

A hearty winter lunch or starter to wash down with a pilsener. The fragrant hops and bitter bite in the beer go well with pickled meats.

1 To make the terrine, brush a terrine mould with the clarified butter and carefully line with the bacon. Mix together the onion and parsley in a bowl and season with pepper. Slice the veal lengthways and using a rolling pin beat out to 3 mm thick. Assemble the terrine by starting with a layer of veal covering the surface of the terrine base, then a layer of the onion mix followed by a layer of bacon. Continue layering until the terrine is full, finishing with a veal layer. Season as you build with pepper only—the bacon provides salt. Seal the terrine with the overlapping bacon. Pour the chicken stock over the terrine and lay the bay leaves on the bacon and cover with a lid.

2 Cook the terrine in a baking dish of simmering water in a preheated oven at 170°C for 1½ hours. Allow to cool before placing enough weight on top to compress the terrine to a slicing consistency but not enough to squeeze out all the meat juices. Refrigerate.

3 To make the piccalilli, place the cauliflower, onion and golden shallots in a bowl and sprinkle with salt. Leave covered in the refrigerator for 24 hours. Rinse in cold water and dry, then add the cucumber to the cauliflower and onion. Boil the two vinegars together with the chilli in a large saucepan over a medium heat. Leave to cool for 1 hour before passing through a fine sieve. Discard the chilli.

4 Mix the sugar and the remaining dry ingredients together in a bowl. When the vinegars are cool mix a little into the dry ingredients to form a paste. Whisk the paste into the remainder of the vinegar until blended together. Bring this mixture back to the boil over a medium heat and cook for 3 minutes. Remove from the heat and add the vegetables. Allow to cool. Place into sterilised jars. To serve, slice the terrine, place it in the centre of a plate and surround with the piccalilli vegetables.

Terrine

¼ **cup clarified butter**
1.4 **kg bacon, rinds removed and sliced**
3 **large onions, diced**
1 **large bunch fresh parsley, finely chopped**
Freshly ground white pepper
4 **veal fillets, trimmed of all fat and sinew**
⅔ **cup chicken stock**
2 **fresh bay leaves**

Piccalilli

1 **cauliflower, cut into florets**
3 **large onions, cut into large dice**
8 **golden shallots, cut into 1 cm dice**
1 **tablespoon salt**
1 **Lebanese cucumber, peeled, deseeded and cut into 1 cm dice**
2⅓ **cups white wine vinegar**
1¼ **cups malt vinegar**
¼ **teaspoon chopped chilli**
1⅓ **cups castor sugar**
2 **tablespoons dry English mustard powder**
½ **tablespoon ground turmeric**
3 **tablespoons cornflour**

Terrine serves 10, piccalilli makes 1.25 kg

Carol Selva Rajah
Beer and spice, a blessed partnership

I HAVE been able to look at beer from a different perspective having been born and brought up in Malaysia where beer was always the drink we served with spicy local food. Beer always worked well in this partnership and it was a comfortable and refreshing drink that complemented the spices, and added a pleasant element to the whole dining experience.

When I arrived in Australia in the early 1970s and found that wine was quickly becoming the drink of choice on Australian tables I found it difficult to understand this move. Wine worked well with European and modern Australian dishes but as Australia progressed toward the spicier flavours of South East and North Asian cuisine, I felt that the oft-suggested sweeter wines like the Gewurtztraminers did not meet the flavours of this cuisine and that the dining experience was being sacrificed for 'fashion'.

Drinking beer with food is an age-old tradition in Asia, despite the influence of the British Raj when civil servants, after a strenuous day of empire building, would gather in Government clubs and rest houses for the 'stenga', a half measure of whisky, or a gin sling at sundown. But even then the Brits showed common sense when it came to dinner. If curry was on the menu, they would turn to Tiger, Anchor or Singha beers just like the locals.

My memories of restaurant meals in Malaysia are of foaming glasses of beer with their clinking ice cubes. In those days beer was the only alcoholic drink appreciated by the local population apart from brandy, quaffed down as the 'yam-seng' toast at weddings. There was very little choice of beer, unlike the tremendous variety available today. Consider the sparkling lagers, rich, creamy stouts, tangy bitters and crisp, clean cold-filtered beers, and—this is particularly relevant to the partnership with spices—a range of fruity beers and 'dessert' beers with rich chocolatey notes.

When matching beer with food, as with wine, it helps to bear in mind that heavily spiced food goes with full-flavoured and robust drinks and lighter, lime-flavoured, piquant dishes go well with the lighter, crisp flavours of milder beers with less noticeable hopping. There is a natural synergy with beer and spices, a natural pairing or coupling of tastes; when their flavours come together they produce layers of deliciously subtle interactions.

There is a natural synergy with beer and spices, a natural pairing or coupling of tastes; when their flavours come together they produce layers of deliciously subtle interactions.

It is all very well to say that one reaches for a glass of something cold when eating a spicy meal. Rather than reaching for a drink to douse the heat why not look for something that will enhance the experience. The tongue is a sensual organ, stimulated by what we eat or drink. Dr Max Lake, author of that great classic, *Food and Wine Flavour—the pleasures of the shared table*, calls the tongue a taste centre and describes it as a toolbox. We use this 'taste centre' or 'toolbox' by providing contrasts that will 'lift' or 'match' the food.

Asian food tradition emphasises the fact that each dish has to have elements of contrast. Flavours such as sweet must contrast with sour. Salty and bitter flavours taste better on the tongue when counterbalanced with taste sensations from the opposite end of the flavour spectrum. The ideal occurs when one flavour simply brings out the other and when the element of surprise adds interest. These flavours are present in all Asian food, sometimes in one dish and at other times in different dishes within the whole meal. As well as a contrast in flavours, there are usually contrasts and complements in textures. Within the one dish there may be crunchy morsels of food to complement 'soft' ingredients and in other dishes, smooth, velvety elements to complement crunch. Beer, too, satisfies the natural desire for contrasts with its mix of malt, nuttiness, caramel, bitterness and spice.

The clink of an ice cube in a beer glass is not uncommon in Asia where a cooling beer is often served at table.

When I cook I enjoy matching my dishes with interesting beers. With a glass of beer and a plate of freshly cooked, spicy food you are aiming to enjoy and appreciate the taste of both. First taste a spoonful, eat and then swallow and sip some beer. When the match is just right, both food and drink will taste better, the food having a sharper taste and the beer presenting its range of flavours from sweet to sour, astringent to bitter.

Always taste and enjoy, then look for reactions. The effervescence refreshes the tongue, and when you swallow, a sweet, slightly malty, astringent taste, and finally a clean bitter flavour, is felt at the back of the tongue. This helps to 'reset' the tongue for the next mouthful and you will find yourself reaching in anticipation for another taste. This remarkable tasting experience is unique to drinking beer with Asian food.

Beer's fermentation process gives it a base note against which all the other spicy flavours play; for example, the yeasty, bitter characters against the aromatics of the curry. Also, beer's volume, intensity, coldness and its soothing, pleasantly alcoholic content matches so much of the blending and 'fermenting' process that takes place in the cooking of spicy food.

Some of the spicy ingredients for Carol Selva Rajah's Chili ketam (Chilli crab). For the recipe see page 94.

Beer picks up the sour notes in tamarind-based dishes like tom yam soups and laksa noodle dishes when big, bold flavours create a partnership of tastes, not vying for attention, but blending beautifully on the palate. Even a tossed omelette with strong-tasting chilli, garlic, chives and onion, when eaten with the bitterness of a mid-strength beer, will leave the diner with a pleasant, cleansing aftertaste, giving the whole dish a particular elegance.

Most Western dishes have a smoothness of texture the whole way through the dish, whereas Asian food has other elements. Flavour 'bursts', bits of chilli or onion in rather large chunks, acting as highlights, add to the main flavour of the dish. The refreshing bite of an accompanying beer takes the flavour of the food to an even higher plane.

Asian food, by its very nature, has a complexity of flavours that are difficult to match with a liquid accompaniment and the aromas with which such food is associated are often impenetrable by good wine. In particular, chilli has a reputation as a wrecker of flavour matches.

Dave DeWitt in his *Chilli Pepper Encyclopaedia*, suggests that chilli desensitises the taste buds through its capsaicin content. Many ingredients have been proposed as an antidote to the heat of chilli, including milk, sugar, citrus fruit, bread and yoghurt. The burning effect of chilli is not dowsed even by water, which provides initial cooling and then serves to spread the volatile oils of the chilli throughout the mouth, adding to the discomfort. The best antidote to a searing hot chilli is a cold beer: the alcohol provides the ingredient in which capsaicin is most soluble and the flavours refresh and revive the palate.

The burn certainly knocks mouth-taste about for a while. However the bitter notes in beer calm the taste buds and the spices react with the bubbles in the beer, lightening up the tongue. Similarly, when sweet and sour dishes are too strong and tire the taste buds, extra bitter beers can counteract this effect, activating digestion and taste buds.

Remember when eating spicy dishes to take a mouthful of food, chew slowly and then swallow. Sip some beer and swirl it around the mouth and then taste. The beer will sit well on the palate when the match is just right and the flavours of both food and beer should appear sharper and clearer.

When serving beer with Asian food I always feel in harmony with the traditions of Asia; sometimes I even think that Asian food might have been created for beer. The dishes that I serve are always different in spice and heat strength and come from the three different regions in Asia, but I always feel that the food has been created with a partnership in mind—the beer for the food and the food for the beer.

What better synergy?

Robert Castellani, Donovan's

Chicken with beer

An old-fashioned recipe similar to coq au vin but cooked in beer rather than wine and then flavoured with gin instead of brandy. Serve with plain boiled potatoes.

1 Heat the butter and oil in a large frying pan over a medium heat. Fry the chicken pieces until golden, in two batches if necessary. Carefully pour off the fat, leaving the chicken in the pan. Add the gin to the pan and deglaze. Carefully light the gin, shaking the pan until the flames die down. Pour in the ale, then add the garlic and herbs. Season with salt and pepper and add the sugar to taste. Cover the pan and simmer for 45 minutes over the lowest heat. Insert a fine skewer into the thickest piece of the chicken. It is cooked when the juices run out clear, not pink. Place the pieces on a warm serving platter, cover and keep warm.

2 Add the button mushrooms to the cooking liquid and cook over a high heat until it is reduced by half. Stir in the crème fraîche. Adjust the final seasoning with sugar and salt and pour the sauce over the chicken.

60 g butter
2 tablespoons oil
1 x 1.5 kg free-range organic chicken, cut into 8 pieces
2 tablespoons gin
1⅓ cups ale
1 garlic clove
Sprig fresh parsley
Fresh bay leaf
Sprig fresh thyme
Salt and freshly ground black pepper
2 teaspoons brown sugar
150 g button mushrooms, sliced
2 tablespoons crème fraîche

Serves 4

Janet Jeffs, Juniperberry
Sparkling ale bread pie

This delicious pie, which incorporates a sparkling ale into its bread case, is filled with savoury pecorino cheese, anchovy, onion, tomatoes and olives—just the dish for a weekend lunch sitting around a fire or for a picnic.

1 To make the bread, sift the flour into a mixing bowl. Dissolve the yeast in the warm water. Make a well in the middle of the flour, add the yeast, water, ale and salt. Stir the flour into the liquid then knead well until the dough is a cohesive and pliable form. Place in a clean bowl and cover with a clean tea towel. Leave it in a warm place to rise to double its size while you prepare the pie filling.

2 Divide the bread dough into 2 equal parts and roll into 2 rounds of equal size, about 1 cm thick. Brush a baking tray with olive oil and lay one round of dough on it. Cover the dough with the slices of cheese, anchovy, ham, onion, tomato, olives, salt and pepper. Top with the second round of dough and press the edges firmly together. Prick the top with a fork and brush with oil. Bake in a preheated oven at 180–200°C for 30–40 minutes until golden brown. Serve hot or at room temperature.

Bread

4 cups (1 kg) baker's flour
10 g dried yeast
⅓ cup warm water
1½ cups sparkling ale
Salt

Olive oil

Pie filling

125 g pecorino cheese, cut into thin slices
6 anchovies
125 g ham, cut into strips
1 onion, sliced
3 large tomatoes, peeled and chopped
15 black olives, pitted
Salt and freshly ground black pepper

Serves 6

Old-fashioned tavern talk

The culture of beer has entered our language through the many sayings that originated in early taverns. The meanings have sometimes changed over time.

Barmy Barm was an old brewing term for the head on beer. So to be barmy is to have a head full of bubbles.

Balderdash This describes a useless mixture of drinks such as a mix of wine and beer.

Bridal Bridal originally referred to bride ale, which was brewed and dispensed by the bride's family in exchange for wedding gifts.

Robert Castellani, Donovan's

Braised oxtail casserole

I have used a stout to enhance this rich oxtail braise. A delicious accompaniment is horseradish potatoes.

2 whole oxtails

⅔ cup vegetable oil

1 teaspoon salt

3 garlic cloves, roughly chopped

2 celery stalks, roughly chopped

1 fresh bay leaf

Sprig fresh thyme

⅔ cup red wine vinegar

4 teaspoons castor sugar

1¾ cups stout

7 cups chicken stock

4 cups beef stock

Freshly ground black pepper

1 tablespoon cornflour

Horseradish potatoes

1 kg good waxy potatoes

⅔ cup cream

60 g butter

2 tablespoons freshly grated horseradish

Salt and freshly ground black pepper

Serves 8

1 Preheat the oven to 190°C. Trim the fat off the oxtails. Make sure the oxtails are cut into portions between the tail joints. Place the portions in a roasting pan and sprinkle them with the oil and salt. Roast them in the oven until brown all over, about 25 minutes.

2 Lift the oxtails out of the pan with a slotted spoon. Add the garlic, celery and herbs and cook in the oven until golden, about 30 minutes at the same temperature.

3 Leaving the vegetables in the pan, deglaze with the vinegar and sugar on top of the stove over a high heat. Reduce the liquid by ⅔. Add 1 cup of the stout and 1 cup of the chicken stock then reduce by half.

4 Put the oxtails back in the pan and cover with the chicken and beef stock. Cover the pan with foil and cook in the oven for 3 hours at 150°C.

5 When cooked, remove the oxtails and strain the vegetables so the liquid falls back into the pan. Reduce the cooking liquid on top of the stove over a high heat until it has thickened enough to coat the back of a spoon. Add the remaining stout and bring to the boil. Adjust the seasoning to taste and add a little more sugar if it is bitter. Sprinkle the cornflour over and stir until the sauce has thickened. Place the oxtails back in the sauce and cook gently until reheated, about 10 minutes.

6 Make the horseradish potatoes while the oxtail is cooking. Boil the potatoes in their skins in simmering water until cooked, about 25 minutes. Drain in a colander and peel off the skins. Pass the potatoes through a sieve or ricer into a bowl. Gradually add the cream and butter, fluffing up the mixture with a wooden spoon as you mix. Add the grated horseradish and season to taste. Commence adding the cream with restraint—you may not need it all. Keep in a warm place until ready to serve. It may be reheated over a low heat with a little extra cream.

Janni Kyritsis, MG Garage

Beef carbonnade

I had a wonderful beef carbonnade in a Belgian restaurant in Paris called Bouillon Racine. I was fascinated by the number of dishes that can be cooked with beer and the immense list of beers on the menu. I have tried many different versions but the following is the one I like to serve.

1 Cook the onions in half the oil in a frying pan over a low heat until soft and well browned, about 30 minutes. Salt and pepper the beef. Brown it in batches in the remaining olive oil in a direct-heat casserole, keeping the heat at medium. Remove the last batch of meat with a slotted spoon and stir in the sugar to caramelise. Stir in the flour and cook for a few minutes. Add the beer and stir, then add the stock and bring it back to the boil. Add the onions, bay leaves, thyme and beef and bring to the boil again. Seal the pan with foil and place the lid on top. Cook in a preheated oven at 150°C for about 2½ hours. Remove from the oven and skim the fat from the top with a spoon and absorbent paper.

2 Adjust the seasoning to taste and serve with vegetables of your choice.

500 g onions, peeled and sliced
⅓ cup olive oil
2 teaspoons salt
2 teaspoons freshly ground black pepper
1.5 kg trimmed and cubed gravy beef
2 teaspoons sugar
3 tablespoons flour
1½ cups lager
1 cup good quality beef stock
3 bay leaves
3 sprigs thyme

Serves 6

'Cooking with beer has always fascinated me. The Belgians use it in numerous dishes. The Irish make lovely stews using Guinness and, indeed, beer is used in many cuisines around the world. One of the most popular uses for beer in my cooking is for batter, which I use constantly in both of my restaurants.'

Janni Kyritsis, MG Garage

Martin Boetz, Longrain

Braised beef shin with a hot and sour salad

A slow-cooked braised beef dish just perfect to wash down with a malty pilsener that has a hint of sweetness balanced by bitterness.

Braising liquid

150 g garlic cloves, peeled
100 g fresh ginger, peeled
6 fresh coriander roots, scraped and cleaned
2 large red onions, chopped
1 tablespoon salt
¾ cup vegetable oil
⅓ cup Chinese cooking wine
80 g rock candy, crushed (Asian food stores)
¾ cup oyster sauce
5 cups chicken stock or 5 cups water with pig's trotter added

Braised beef

1 cup vegetable oil
4 x 200 g beef shin pieces
⅓ cup ABC sweet soy sauce (ketchup manis) or similar
4 tablespoons Chinese black vinegar

Hot and sour dressing

⅓ cup lime juice
1 teaspoon red chilli powder
2 tablespoons fish sauce
3 small green chillies, finely sliced

Salad

½ cup fresh coriander leaves
½ cup fresh mint leaves
3 spring onions, finely shredded
4 red shallots, finely sliced
1 large red chilli, deseeded and finely sliced

Serves 4–6

1 To make the braising liquid, pound the garlic, ginger, coriander, red onion and salt to a paste in a mortar and pestle or food processor. In a heavy-based saucepan over a medium heat add the oil and fry the pounded ingredients until golden brown. Pour off the excess oil and deglaze the pan with the Chinese cooking wine, adding the crushed rock candy and oyster sauce. Stir and pour the chicken stock over. Bring to the boil and skim the surface clean.

2 To braise the beef, place the oil in a wok and heat over a high heat until very hot, about 280°C. Check with a bread cube—if it turns golden brown within 1 minute it is ready. Rub the beef shin with the soy. Deep-fry each piece individually until golden brown, about 40 seconds. Drain and place in a deep casserole dish. Pour the braising liquid over the beef and cover with a tight-fitting lid.

3 Braise for 3 hours in a preheated oven at 180°C. Remove the meat from the braising liquid and set aside. Strain the braising liquid into a saucepan and reduce the liquid over a high heat. Add the Chinese black vinegar to cut the richness. Adjust the seasoning by adding salt or sugar.

4 To make the hot and sour salad, mix the lime juice, chilli powder and fish sauce together and add the finely-sliced green chillies. The dressing should taste very hot and sour. Toss the salad ingredients in a bowl with the dressing.

5 To serve, cut the braised beef into 1 cm slices and reheat in the reduced braising liquor. Place some sliced beef in the centre of each serving bowl, generously pouring over some braising liquid. Place the hot and sour salad on top of the beef, pouring some of the hot and sour dressing into the meaty liquor. Serve with steamed rice.

Margaret Fulton, *New Idea*

Steak and kidney pie with beer and mushrooms

Steak and kidney pie with its rich, thick, peppery gravy is classic, hearty fare that remains a nourishing, economical dish for serving to family and friends on a chilly night. The golden puff pastry crust seals in the aromatic juices whether topping one pie or individual ones. The ale introduces a malt sweetness and a citrusy hop character. A complex amber ale goes well with a rich meat pie.

Steak and kidney

- 1 calf's kidney or 2–3 sheep's kidneys
- 1 kg chuck or blade steak, cut into 2.5 cm cubes
- 1 tablespoon flour + extra
- 1 teaspoon salt
- 1 teaspoon freshly ground black pepper
- 2 teaspoons chopped fresh thyme and parsley leaves
- ½ cup ale
- 2 anchovy fillets, chopped
- ¼ teaspoon ground nutmeg
- 125 g mushrooms, sliced

- 1 x 375 g packet frozen puff pastry, thawed
- Egg yolk, beaten with a little water, to make egg glaze

Serves 6

1 Remove the cores from the kidney with a sharp knife—they are the fatty white bits. Slice the kidney roughly.

2 Sprinkle the meat and kidney with flour, salt, pepper and herbs. Spoon into a heavy saucepan and pour the ale over. Cover tightly and simmer very gently over a low heat for about 2 hours, or in a preheated slow oven at 160°C for about 2½ hours or until the meat is tender. If necessary, add a little more ale.

3 When cooked, stir in the anchovies, nutmeg and the mushrooms. Allow to cool.

4 Spoon the cooked steak and kidney mixture into a pie dish just large enough to hold it, mounding it up in the centre (to hold pastry up). A pie funnel, often in the shape of a blackbird, can be placed in the centre of the meat to hold the pastry up and keep it crisp in the centre. Allow the meat to cool, if not already.

5 Roll out the pastry dough on a lightly floured board to 2.5 cm larger all round than the top of the dish. Cut off a strip of dough all around, 2.5 cm wide, and place the strip on the edge of the dish. Brush with a little egg glaze and cover with the dough round or oval. Press firmly onto the strip to seal and then trim the edges with a knife. Cut an air vent (about 1 cm round) in the centre of the dough lid to let the steam escape when cooking. Decorate with a pastry rose and leaves, if liked. Chill for 30 minutes.

6 Brush the pie with the egg glaze to make the pastry golden and shiny. Bake in a preheated oven at 200°C for 20–30 minutes. Reduce the heat to 180°C and bake for a further 30–40 minutes. It may be necessary to cover the pastry with foil to prevent over-browning.

9. The icing on the cake: desserts

Genevieve Harris, Nediz

Vanilla ice cream with chocolate stout sauce and malt praline

The malt used to produce stout is dark roasted to produce chocolate, coffee and nut flavours, making it is a natural choice to accompany this dessert. The dish includes these flavours as well as blending ice cream to complement the texture and taste of a full-bodied stout.

Vanilla ice cream

2½ cups cream

1⅓ cups milk

1 vanilla bean, split and seeds scraped out

8 egg yolks

⅔ cup castor sugar

Chocolate malt praline

Hazelnut oil

3 tablespoons chocolate malt (available from home-brewing stores)

1⅓ cups castor sugar

⅔ cup water

Chocolate stout sauce

125 g dark chocolate

50 g butter

3 tablespoons icing sugar

⅔ cup full-bodied stout

Serves 6–8

1 To make the ice cream, place the cream, milk, vanilla bean and seeds in a large saucepan. Place over a low heat and bring it almost to the boil. Remove from the heat. Whisk the egg yolks and castor sugar together until light and creamy in texture. Slowly pour the hot cream mixture into the egg mixture, whisking continuously. Place the egg-cream mixture over a saucepan of just simmering water and stir until the mixture thickens to a custard consistency. Strain through a fine sieve. Cool then churn in an ice-cream machine according to the manufacturer's instructions.

2 To make the praline, lightly oil a metal tray with the hazelnut oil and sprinkle the chocolate malt over the tray. In a small saucepan dissolve the sugar and the water over a low heat. Simmer this sugar syrup until it changes colour to golden brown. Pour it over the tray with the chocolate malt. Allow to cool, then crush it with a mortar and pestle. Store the praline in the freezer until required.

3 To make the sauce, melt the chocolate and butter in a stainless steel bowl over a saucepan of just simmering water. Add the icing sugar and stout and whisk to combine. Set aside and keep warm until serving.

4 To serve, scoop the vanilla ice cream into sundae glasses or ice cream bowls. Pour warm chocolate stout sauce over, sprinkle with chocolate malt praline and a sweet biscuit if liked. Serve immediately with a glass of chilled stout.

Previous page: Genevieve Harris's Vanilla ice cream with chocolate stout sauce and malt praline.

Gary Miller, Christchurch Casino

Rice and barley pudding with fresh berry compote

Stout is ideal to drink with this dessert. The contrast of sweetness, the bitterness of hops and the drink's smooth velvety texture harmonise with the creamy rice. A true beer and food marriage!

1 To make the pudding, gently heat the cream and milk in a saucepan over a low heat. Just before it comes to the boil add the sugar and stir. When it is dissolved add the two rices and the pearl barley. Stir thoroughly until all the dry ingredients are evenly coated with cream. Simmer for 5 minutes, stirring occasionally.

2 Transfer the rice mixture to a warm oven-proof dish and bake, covered, in a preheated oven at 190°C for 30 minutes.

3 To make the compote, place the berries and the sugar in a saucepan and gently bring to a simmer. Add the star anise. Leave to simmer for 20 minutes, stirring occasionally. Once cooked to coating consistency remove the star anise.

4 To serve, spoon the pudding into the centre of four warm dessert bowls. Spoon the berry compote on top of the pudding and drizzle the berry juice around the base of the pudding. Garnish with fresh mint tips.

Pudding

¾ cup cream

1¼ cups milk

2 tablespoons soft brown sugar

½ cup shortgrain rice

¼ cup wild rice, soaked overnight

½ cup pearl barley, soaked overnight

Compote

500 g fresh or frozen mixed berries such as raspberries, blackberries and blueberries

1 tablespoon soft brown sugar, optional

1 star anise

Fresh mint tips to garnish

Serves 4

Yet more tavern talk

Cock and bull story Once upon a time there were two taverns on a main road to London, the Cock and the Bull. While the coaching horses rested, passengers in the taverns drank ale, and told exaggerated tales of the fame and fortune to be had in London—these soon became known as 'cock and bull' stories.

Honeymoon A honey-infused beer was given to newlyweds for the first month (moon) of their marriage to encourage fertility—hence the term honeymoon.

George Diamond, Siggi's
Dark valhrona chocolate tart

The stout in the tart's sabayon accompaniment highlights the characteristics of the chocolate while the intense sweetness of the prunes balances any bitterness.

1 To make the macerated prunes, put all the ingredients—except the prunes—in a saucepan and bring to the boil over a medium heat. Add the prunes and remove from the heat. Store in a sterilised jar. Prepare one week in advance.
2 To make the pastry, mix the flour, sugar, lemon zest and salt together in a bowl. Rub the butter into the flour mixture with your fingers until it resembles breadcrumbs. Gradually add just enough water to the flour mixture until the pastry is blended and will hold together when you press it. Form the pastry into a ball and wrap in cling film. Rest for 30 minutes. Press the pastry out evenly into a 28 cm tart tin. Freeze the pastry shell for 30 minutes.
3 Preheat the oven to 190°C and blind bake the shell for 20–25 minutes or until baked through. To bake blind, loosely line the shell with baking paper and fill with rice or dried beans. Remove the paper and weights when cooked.
4 To make the tart filling, melt the 2 chocolates, cocoa and butter in a bowl sitting on top of a saucepan of simmering water. Stir with a spoon until lump free. In a separate bowl, whisk the sugar, eggs and egg yolks with an electric beater until light and fluffy. Gently fold ⅓ of this mixture into the chocolate mixture. Knock the air out of the remaining sugar-egg mixture to stop it rising in the cooking process then fold the chocolate mixture into it. Stir only until evenly coloured. Place the chocolate filling in the pastry case and bake in the preheated oven at 170°C for 30 minutes.
5 To make the sabayon, whisk all the ingredients in a stainless steel bowl sitting over a saucepan of simmering water. Continue to whisk until the mixture is light and fluffy. Store in a warm place.
6 To serve, place a wedge of the warm tart on a serving plate. Spoon a little of the sabayon on to the tart followed by 2 prunes. Drizzle with the prune syrup.

Macerated prunes for 4
¼ cup water
¼ cup sugar
1½ tablespoons Armagnac
1 stick cinnamon
8 prunes, pitted

Pastry
1½ cups plain flour
1 tablespoon sugar
¼ teaspoon lemon zest
¼ teaspoon salt
185 g butter, softened and diced
1 tablespoon water

Tart filling
185 g valhrona dark chocolate
155 g valhrona milk chocolate
¼ cup cocoa powder
185 g butter
¼ cup sugar
4 eggs
4 egg yolks

Sabayon for 4
2 egg yolks
3 tablespoons brown sugar
¼ cup full-strength, highly hopped stout

Accompaniment serves 4, tart serves 12

Richard Thomas

Cheese and beer marriages

A fine blue cheese, oatmeal biscuits and a restorative beer make a comforting, traditional end to dinner on a winter's evening.

BEER is very democratic and knows no social boundaries. And in moderate amounts, it makes an excellent social lubricant, particularly at the end of a day's work. On top of this beer seems to find a comfortable place amongst all company, foods and flavours. Beer demands so much less attention and fuss than wine, its only liquid equivalent, and is much more content just to be drunk, accompanying any sort of food.

The history of cheese and beer is as one. Both were accidents of nature, harnessed by human experience and ingenuity. The principal fermentation of sugar by yeasts and bacteria is shared by both. Like all foods preserved by fermentation—and here we can talk of olives, anchovies, salami as well as beer, wine and cheese—they have an affinity for each other. Not only in a flavour sense, but nutritionally. All these foods are pre-digested; the yeasts and bacteria break them down into simpler components, and they are readily absorbed by the body. More importantly, the bacteria used in these fermentations are a great aid to the digestion of food within the gut itself.

Immoderate amounts of all these foods are consumed within all traditional cultures; the testimony to their benefits is the generally lower incidence of diseases in the heart and other vital organs. Essential fatty and amino acids are in plentiful supply in these fermented foods, beer and cheese being prime and justifiably popular examples.

Beer and cheese share other distinctions. Every day is a 'vintage' day to the brewer and to the cheesemaker, at the end of which, without ever thinking about it, each enjoys the others' harvest. Both are workers in food. Workers have no time to spare on the vagaries of bouquet, middle-palate flavours and the like, in high-falutin' language—they're too busy enjoying the moment, the relaxation and the drink.

Beer is a mighty fluid, only water slakes thirst more thoroughly than beer. This makes me think about the importance of actually building up a thirst, and salt does that. And that's where cheese comes into the picture. Fetta is probably the most briny cheese, so it must be a perfect bedmate for beer I would say. Yes, what a fine combination—fetta, wild peppery rocket and a very cold beer.

When it comes to salt and thirst, French roquefort, salty as hell, should marry with beers possessing malty sweetness. I have found this to be so. English ploughmen found cheddar and warm beer were fine together, and English beer is often fruity, plump, almost sweet—not unlike their cheese. Even if we don't go for this combination ourselves, have we the right to question the merits of a tradition some hundred or so years old?

Beer was commonly quaffed by the British at breakfast and Welsh rarebit and its variations include beer or stout. But use only the sweeter stouts of the Scottish kind rather than the more well-known bitter stouts, Guinness for example. Further east, the Poles would often start the day with a beer and curd cheese soup. In fact, recognising the warming and nutritional qualities of both foods, many cold climate countries have, over time, produced a range of dishes containing beer and cheese.

The histories of cheese and beer go back many thousands of years. Cheeses, mead, wine and beer go back to Babylonian times and were said to be plentiful in both ancient Egypt and ancient Rome and, eventually, across their empires.

Monks brought more than just religious enlightenment in the days when they occupied a prominent place in society. We often see cheeses and beers named after monasteries where they originated; and in some cases they are still produced. Of the cheeses, washed rind styles were predominantly made by the monks. The monks of Ireland took their precious washed rind molines recipe to Europe and the general belief is that munster is still made to their recipe—and is often accompanied by beer.

I find that soft and musky cheeses, the likes of camembert and washed rind styles, are assuredly less compatible to serve with wine and so it is with beer. Firstly, beer that is too cold creates an unpleasant feeling in the mouth, the fat in the cheese solidifies and a soapy bitterness prevails. My moral of this story is: I prefer to serve hard cheese with beer, either cheddar or the Italian varieties. Nevertheless, why not experiment and see what suits your taste.

There has been for me, a longstanding rule for cheese and wine—sugar will help marry their flavours. That is, sweet wines or fruit are the marriage celebrants. Sweetness in beer has pretty much the same effect. For example, there are those—and I am one of them—who say that under no circumstances (unless you're Irish) should you serve stout with cheese. On the other hand, some find this combination another happy beer and cheese marriage.

The most heartening news for lovers of good food and drink is that every occasion is fine for beer and cheese, and there is certainly a beer and a cheese for every occasion.

Every day is a 'vintage' day to the brewer and to the cheesemaker, at the end of which, without ever thinking about it, each enjoys the others' harvest.

Crumbled fetta cheese and rocket (arugula) sprinkled with olive oil and a grinding of pepper demands to be washed down with a crisp, cold beer.

Tony Bilson, chef and food writer

Stout sorbet

Serve this sorbet alone or with a pudding with neutral flavours. A simple bread and butter pudding would be perfect or simply a sweet biscuit.

⅔ **cup castor sugar**

2 **cups stout**

2½ **tablespoons lemon juice**

Serves 4–6

1 Dissolve the sugar in the stout in a large bowl. It will foam when sugar is first added so make sure there is room for expansion. Add the lemon juice and place in an ice-cream churn and churn according to the manufacturer's instructions. It you don't have a churn, freeze the mixture overnight and then blend it in a blender or food processor until it has a creamy consistency, then return to the freezer.

Robert Castellani, Donovan's

Mother-in-law's cake

My mother-in-law Patricia made this cake for me and it was so delicious I had to pass it on. A rich porter adds good flavour while keeping the cake moist.

225 g butter

1⅓ **cup soft brown sugar**

4 eggs, lightly beaten

2⅓ **cups plain flour, sieved with the spice**

2 teaspoons mixed spice

1⅓ **cups seedless raisins**

1¼ **cups sultanas**

¾ **cup mixed peel**

1 cup walnuts, chopped

1¼ **cups porter**

Serves 12

1 Preheat the oven to 160°C. Use a 16 cm ring tin—grease and line your cake tin with baking paper if necessary.

2 Cream the butter and sugar together with electric beaters until light and creamy. Gradually beat in the eggs. Gently fold in the flour and mixed spice with a wooden spoon. Add the raisins, sultanas, mixed peel and walnuts, mixing with care. Stir ½ cup of porter into the mixture until it has a soft, dough-like consistency.

3 Turn the cake batter into the ring tin, smoothing the surface with a spatula. Bake in the preheated oven for 1 hour. Reduce the heat to 150°C and cook for another 1½ hours. Test for doneness with a fine skewer. When it comes out clean it is cooked.

4 Allow the cake to cool in the tin, then remove to a plate. Peel the paper off if necessary. Prick the base with a fine skewer and spoon over the remaining porter. Keep the cake sealed in a cake tin for 1 week before eating. Serve with a rich pure cream and perhaps some poached fruits. A glass of porter goes well.

David Pugh, II (two)
Drunken fruit steamed pudding

Best eaten with a flute of stout. The stout and the pudding have the same smooth mouthfeel while the spices in the pudding complement the flavour of the stout. The drunken fruit is best made one month in advance.

Drunken fruit

4 cups sugar

1 cinnamon stick

1 cup dried figs, roughly chopped

½ cup prunes, pitted, roughly chopped

⅔ cup dried currants

½ cup sultanas

½ cup raisins

3 tablespoons mixed peel

2½ tablespoons rum

2½ tablespoons brandy

Steamed pudding

2 large eggs

90 g unsalted butter + extra

½ cup castor sugar

1⅓ cups self-raising flour, sifted

⅓ cup almond meal

1 teaspoon baking powder

½ tablespoon ground cinnamon

1 tablespoon mixed spice

⅕ cup milk

400 g drunken fruit

Double cream or ice cream to serve

Serves 6–8

1 Make the drunken fruit 1 month in advance for best results. Make a sugar syrup by dissolving the sugar in 2 cups of water with the cinnamon stick over a medium heat. Add all the dried fruit to it and reduce the heat to a simmer for 10 minutes. Stir gently. Remove from the heat, add the alcohol, stir and allow to cool. Store in an airtight glass container in the refrigerator.

2 To make the steamed puddings, separate the egg yolks and whites. Whip the egg whites to a soft, pale consistency. Cream the butter and sugar with electric beaters until pale and fluffy. Slowly add the egg yolks with the beaters on low speed. Then slowly add the self-raising flour, almond meal, baking powder, cinnamon and mixed spice. With a wooden spoon stir in the milk and ⅔ of the drunken fruit. Fold in the egg whites with the spoon being careful not to overstir. Spoon into individual buttered pudding moulds until ⅔ full. Cover each pudding lightly with buttered foil.

3 Place the puddings, well separated, in a large baking tray and gently pour in boiling water until 2 cm deep. Cook in a preheated oven at 180°C for 30 minutes or until done. Insert a fine skewer and when it comes out clean it is ready. Remove the puddings from the oven and water-bath. Cool for 10 minutes. Warm the remaining drunken fruit gently in a small saucepan. Turn the puddings out of their moulds and serve topped with the remaining drunken fruit. Serve with double cream or ice cream.

The track o' life is dry enough an' crossed with many a rut, But oh we'll find it longer still when all the pubs is shut.

Henry Lawson

Biographies

Barbara Beckett grew up trying to emulate her grandmother's good home cooking. She works as an art director and has published numerous books, including a healthy sprinkling of cook books. She has written *Gourmet Gifts*, *The Harvest Pantry* and recently co-authored *Cooking for Dummies*.

Maggie Beer is an enthusiastic supporter of regional food. She built Maggie's Beer Products, SA, into an award-winning range of her farm produce. Maggie has also written more than four fascinating cook books and her latest is the splendid, *Maggie's Table*.

Tony Bilson has been developing his unique cooking style in Sydney for more than 35 years, combining French cuisine, Mediterranean flavours and local seasonal ingredients—food that perfectly suits our environment and lifestyle. Among the restaurants Tony has developed are Berowra Waters and Bilson's (Quay). He is considered one of the leaders of contemporary cuisine.

Martin Boetz's greatest influence was his German grandmother's home-style cooking. He arrived in Sydney at the age of 15 and after working in many kitchens, including Darley St Thai, Martin opened Longrain. His food is a delicate blend of Thai and southern Chinese influences—a journey into Asian-style dining, Australian style.

Joan Campbell calls herself a bush cook. The most important thing to her is to just cook a good dish and have everyone say it's delicious. But few people have been as influential as Joan—she has been a Sydney cookery teacher, caterer and food journalist as well as food director for *Vogue* food publications.

Robert Castellani was born in Pavia and migrated to Australia as a child. 'I am Italian, I live in Australia, my ingredients are Australian—when they are cooked they speak a few words of Italian.' Robert is never afraid to serve well-balanced, simple dishes at Melbourne's Donovan's—he believes simplicity is the key to success.

George Diamond worked as chef at the Brisbane Powerhouse until he moved on to become chef de cuisine at Siggi's in Brisbane. He has created several beer dinners with Bill Taylor—taste his chocolate valhrona tart, page 133, as evidence of a brilliant match.

Peter Doyle of Celsius, Sydney, is affectionately known by his peers as the 'chef's chef'. His fine food is essentially Australian, utilising classic French techniques. Peter's dishes are highly visual—he concentrates on seasonal ingredients and lets the food speak for itself. 'Restraint and simplicity are important qualities for a perfectly cooked dish.'

Len Evans AO OBE washed glasses in a pub before embarking on a career in the wine industry. He was founding director of the Australian Wine Bureau that promoted Australian wines so successfully. By 1996 he was president of the Australian Wine Foundation, initiating the aim to make Australia one of the five great wine nations of the world. Len is a respected international wine judge, a winemaker and a best-selling author.

Alain Fabrègues grew up under the influence of his grandmother, a famous cook in her day. Alain and his wife Elizabeth opened The Loose Box near Perth which has won a staggering number of awards. He is dedicated to producing the finest French cuisine while cultivating and celebrating the wonderful fresh produce of the West.

Sue Fairlie-Cuninghame is a busy food journalist currently working with *Inside Out*. She is also very committed to regionalism, encouraging growers and producers to think laterally and value-add. Sue's work helps improve the qualilty of food and hospitality in country regions.

Margaret Fulton OAM has been instrumental in teaching generations of people not only to cook but to appreciate fine food and high-quality ingredients. She has written a weekly food column in women's magazines for 55 years. Her first book, *Margaret*

Fulton's Cook Book, sold more than a million copies. Part of her success is the ability to simplify the complex and make fine dishes more accessible.

Chuck Hahn is a brewer who is passionate about getting people to 'drink upstream from the herd'. He has a beer named after him and he has won a couple of dozen international awards for boutique brewing. His latest brewing exploits are as founder, director and brewmaster of the Malt Shovel Brewery in Sydney, which makes the James Squire range of beers.

Louise Harper was born in southern India and migrated here with her family when aged 11. After years of teaching cooking she is now chef at Sydney's Oh! Calcutta where she develops new dishes drawn from authentic recipes she collects in India. She reworks them with fresh ingredients to suit our palate and climate.

Genevieve Harris worked in several acclaimed restaurants before returning to her native Adelaide and the well-known Nediz. She is a perfectionist and a chef of 'incredible finesse and refinement.' Genevieve likes to blend Asian and Mediterranean flavours using only the finest ingredients.

Robert Irving is an architect, architectural historian and building conservation consultant. He holds the degree of Master of Architecture from the University of New South Wales, where he also taught architecture for many years. He is author, amongst many others, of *Identifying Australian Architecture* and *Twentieth Century Architecture in Wollongong*.

Janet Jeffs worked with Cheong Liew and Maggie Beer before moving to Canberra to open the very successful Juniperberry. Janet recently moved the restaurant seamlessly to the National Gallery of Australia. Juniperberry is now beautifully sited in the handsome sculpture garden—the ideal home.

Philip Johnson's philosophy is to do as little as possible with the best ingredients available. He opened his bold Brisbane restaurant, e'cco, to packed tables in 1995. His fine-flavoured food has been described as food that makes you feel ten years younger. His second cookbook, *e'cco 2*, has just been published by Random House Australia.

Janni Kyritsis grew up in northern Greece and although he took his basic cooking skills from Greece he describes himself as a Mediterranean-influenced Australian cook. He insists that fine ingredients and flavours are the most important elements of a dish. Diners at Sydney's MG Garage agree!

Cheong Liew grew up in Malaysia, equally at home with Chinese, Malayan and Indian food. His grandmother encouraged him to cook so that when he came to Australia his love of food drew him to the kitchen. Cheong pioneered the fusion of European and Asian cuisines and ingredients—his food at The Grange in Adelaide is unique for its flavour, texture and visual appeal.

Stefano Manfredi migrated from Italy as a young boy and grew up absorbing traditional food culture from his mother and grandmother. Though he has an Italian approach to food he believes the fine fresh Australian ingredients he uses transforms his dishes. He is still working alongside his mother at Sydney's bel mondo.

Lyndey Milan is an infectious communicator about food and wine who brings enthusiasm and passion to her practical and academic interests, whether she is writing a cookbook, steering the food at *The Australian Women's Weekly* or presenting on TV and radio.

Garry Miller has been passionate about food from a tender age. After training and working overseas he settled at Christchurch Casino. Gary has developed special menus for beer and food events for Steinlager, both in New Zealand and overseas. He greatly enjoys demonstrating the versatility of beer and food matching.

Damien Pignolet grew up in Melbourne with a French father and a mother who loved cooking. In Sydney, Damien opened Claudes which soon gained recognition for its exquisite food. He fulfilled another dream by creating the immensely successful Bistro Moncur.

David Pugh ran one of Brisbane's best BYOs restaurants, Two Small

Rooms for years. His use of classic techniques combined with fine ingredients and contemporary flair assured success when he opened the acclaimed II (two) several years ago.

David Sampson trained in London then headed down under to work at the Harbour Restaurant. Currently David is working with Anders Ousbach at Lynwood Stores, Sydney, creating delicious vacuum-packed food and preserves for too-busy-to-cook days.

Carol Selva Rajah was born in Singapore to a Sri Lankan father and Malaysian mother. She developed an early interest in cooking which was honed later in Asia and Australia. Carol works not only as a chef and food writer, but as a TV presenter, speaker, teacher and a guide to Asian Sydney.

Kate Sparrow began studying art but quickly switched to her greater interest, food and wine. She and her partner Le Tu Thai opened Adelaide's renowned Nediz Tu restaurant in the late 1980s. After winning many prestigious awards they moved to a new challenge at Petaluma's The Bridgewater Mill, still working together.

Chris Taylor worked in top hotels in Australia, England and Switzerland until he opened his own acclaimed restaurant Fraser's, in beautiful King's Park in Perth. Chris enthusiastically supports the local produce such as Albany oysters and local game. He travels regularly overseas promoting Western Australian wine and food.

Richard Thomas worked in the dairy industry as a chemist before deciding to branch into cheese-making. 'Gorgonzola inspired me! I couldn't see why we couldn't make decent cheeses instead of cheddar.' His first cheese was Gippsland Blue, an acclaimed and pioneering cheese. Richard has gone on to develop many fine artisan cheeses such as Milawa Washed Rind and Meredith Blue.

Liam Tomlin began his food life in Ireland, honed it in fine hotel kitchens in Europe, then luckily found his way to Australia. After Brasserie Cassis, he became executive chef at Sydney's Banc and Wine Banc. Liam believes in keeping his food simple and concentrating on two or three flavours.

Text sources

Grateful acknowledgement is made to the owners of copyright for permission to use quoted material. Every effort has been made to contact all copyright owners; the publishers would appreciate notification of any omissions or corrections of sources wrongly attributed for inclusion in future editions. Deutsher, Keith M, *The Breweries of Australia*, Lothian, South Melbourne, 1999; Pearl, Cyril, *Beer, Glorious Beer*, Nelson, Melbourne, 1969; Saunders, Lucy, *Cooking with Beer: Taste-Tempting Recipes and Creative Ideas for Matching Beer & Food*, Time-Life Books, Amsterdam, 1996; Slessor, Kenneth, 'Country Towns' in *One Hundred Poems*, Angus & Robertson, Sydney, 1944; Thirkell, Angela, *Trooper to the Southern Cross*, Sun Books, Melbourne, 1966.

Historic illustration sources

NATIONAL LIBRARY OF AUSTRALIA: p 8 *Picnic on the Hawkesbury* c 1890s; p 56 *The First House Built in Melbourne* 1863, WFE Liardet; p 60 *Off to the Diggings* SC Brees, 1856. JOE WHITE MALTINGS: p 15 *Maltsters at work* c 1920; p 54 *Joe White Maltsters* c 1890. Cath Freeland: pp 17, 18, 55, 61, 74 for photographs by JM Freeland, *The Australian Pub*. BAROSSA VALLEY MUSEUM: p 20 *Chop Picnic*. RMN–PHOTO AGENCY: p 49 *Cereal Harvest and Plowing* c 1450 BC, Musée du Louvre. STADTBIBLIOTHEK NÜRNBERG: p 51 *The Brewer Monk*, 1388, Konrad Mendel's *Chronicle*. STAATLICHE KUNSTSAMMLUNGEN DRESDEN: p 53 *Portrait of the Artist with his Wife Saskia* or *The Prodigal Son*, 1636, Rembrandt van Rijn. LA TROBE PICTURE COLLECTION, STATE LIBRARY OF VICTORIA: p 57 *Sly Grog Shanty on the Road to Bendigo* ST Gill, 1852. THE SA BREWING CO: p 58 *West End Brewery*, 1906, *History of the South Australian Brewing Company Limited*.

Antiques in contemporary photographs kindly loaned by John Williams and John Scott. Thanks also to The Bay Tree.

Index

Page numbers in italics indicate illustrations

abbey-style beers 47
Abbot, Edward 15, 21
ale 10, 38–41
   varieties and brand names 39–41
altbier 47
amber ale 40
American lager 46
aperitif 68
Austen, Jane 11

Babylon 49–50, 135
Beckett, Barbara 82, *82*, 83
beef carbonnade 22, 70, *70*, 71
beer
   boutique 43
   brewing 12–13
   cooking with 70–1
   combining with food 21–2, 64–9,
      71–3, 84–5, 118–121
   contents 66
   drinking 24–5, 30–1
   early recipes 11, 14
   fermentation 13, 38
   health benefits of 66
   in Australia 8, 14–15, 17–22, 54–9
   in England 8–11,
   in medieval times 50–52
   ingredients 24, 26–7, 44–5
   lautering 13
   mashing 12
   origins 49–50
   pouring 29–30
   'specialty' varieties 47
   storage 32–3

   tasting 31, 34–5
   wine matches 73
   with spicy dishes 118–121
   with cheese 134–5
beer and food matches 72–3
beer batter 21, 22, *68*, 70, 79, 86, 88, 93, 96
beer brands 35, 37–43, 46–7
beer chutney 83
beer glasses 28–30
Beer, Maggie 22, *68*, 93
Belgian wheat beer 42
bière de garde 47
Bigge, JT 14
Bilson, Tony 21, 84–5, *85*, 93, 116, 136, *137*
bock 46
Boetz, Martin 126, *127*
boutique lager 43
bread pie with sparkling ale *122*, 123
breweries
   boutique 44–5
   history in Australia 54–8
broth *see* soup
brown ale 40

cabbage 116
cake, mother-in-law's 22, 66, *66*, 136
Campbell, Joan 21, 79, 112
carbonnade *see* meat and game
Castellani, Robert 22, *22*, 66, 121, 124, 136
caudle 11
cheese 10, 19, 34, 65, 69, 71–2, 78,

134–135
chicken
   combining with beer 68, 71–2, 84–5
chicken recipes
   à la bière 102–103
   spiced grilled 105
   squid salad 98, *99*
   with beer 121
chillies 120–1
chocolate 22, 67–8, 72, *132*, 133
   in tart 67, *67*, *132*, 133
   with stout sauce, malt praline and
      vanilla ice cream *129*, 130
chop picnic *20*, 21
chops, mutton 16, *20*, 21
coconut chutney 77
colonial beer banter 111
counter lunch 19–20
crostini with peas, roast garlic and
   anchovies 22, *76*, 77

dark ale 40
dark lager 46
Diamond, George 67, *132*, 133
digestif 69
dips
   coconut chutney 77
   dukkah 19, 22, *80*, 81
   muhammara 22, 78
Doyle, Peter *19*, 22, *80*, 81, 86, *87*
dressings *see* sauces
dukkah *19*, *80*, 81

Elizabeth I 9

Egypt 50
Evans, Len 100–101

Fabrègues Alain 104
Fairlie-Cuninghame, Sue 22, 79, 107, *107*
fish
 cooking with beer 70, 72–3
 combining with beer 68–9, 84–5
fish recipes
 cured salmon with cabbage *21*, 116
 flathead in beer batter *68*, 93
 machi pakorhas (fish fritters) 88
 Malaysian ikan sumbat (stuffed fish) 95
 roast red emperor with braised zucchini and a bread and tarragon salsa *89*, 97
 terrine of smoked salmon with crab salad 90, *91*
 whitebait, parsley and pancetta fritters 96
food and beer matches 72–3
framboise 63
fruit
 berry compote 131
 drunken 138
 prunes, macerated 133
Fulton, Margaret 22, 105, 108, 128

game *see* meat
gueuze 47, 53

Hahn, Chuck 12–3, 44–5, 84
Harper, Louise 88, 106, *110*, 111
Harris, Genevieve 22, *129*, 130
Hildegard of Bingen 51

hops 13, 24, *24*, 26, 27, 55, *59*, 60

ice cream, vanilla with chocolate stout sauce and malt praline *129*, 130
Irving, Robert 60–2

Jeffs, Janet *122*, 123
Johnson, Philip *2*, 22, 92

ketchup 11
kriek 47, 72–3
kölsch 47
Kyritsis, Janni 22, *70*, 125

lager 24, 37–8
 introduction of 57–9
 varieties and brand names 42–6
lambic 47, 53
Liew, Cheong 113
light beer 43

Macquarie, Lachlan 14
malt 12, 26
Manfredi, Stefano 22, *76*, 77, *89*, 97
mashing 12
meat and game
 cooking with beer, 70–3, 84–5
 combining with beer 68, 69, 84–5
meat and game recipes
 braised beef shin with a hot and sour salad 126, *127*
 braised oxtail casserole 22, 124
 beef carbonnade 22, 70, *70*, 125
 cloistered rabbit Bohemian 104
 kangaroo sahk dhada 106
 lamb shoulder braised with parsley and ale 22, 114, *115*

lamb with Thai mint dressing 22, 106
 leg of ham baked in stout with spiced peaches 108
 steak and kidney pie with beer and mushrooms 22, 128
 truffle burgers 107, *107*
 veal and bacon terrine 117
Milan, Lyndey 22, 106
Miller, Garry 22, 77, 78, 131
muhammara 22, 78

olives, spicy green *80*, 81
oysters 6, 7, 22, 65, 72, 84, 86, *87*

pale ale 39–40
Pasteur, Louis 52
Pearl, Cyril 56
pickled mango and carrot 98
pie
 sparkling ale and bread *122*, 123
 steak and kidney with beer and mushrooms 128
piccalilli 117
Pignolet, Damien 22, 114, *115*
pilsener 43, 46, 54
porter 40
posset 11, *11*, 14
potatoes, horseradish 124
premium lager 43
Prince Alfred visit (1868) 7
pubs
 advertising 20
 in Australia 60–2, 74–5
 city *18*, 31, 56–7, 62, *62*, 74–5, *75*
 country 17–8, *17*, 55, 56, 60–1, *61*
pudding
 rice and barley with fresh berry

compote 131
steamed drunken fruit 138
Pugh, David 67, *109*, 112, 138

rauchbier 47
red ale 40
rice and barley pudding with fresh berry compote 131

salad
    cooking with beer 73
    combining with beer 68
salad recipes
    chicken and squid 98, *99*
    crab 90
    cuttlefish, pawpaw, chilli, lime and cashews *2*, *22*, 92
    hot and sour 126, *127*
    rice 106
Sampson, David 78, 83, 102, *103*
sauces and dressings
    bread and tarragon 97
    chocolate and stout 130
    gribiche 86
    hot and sour 126
    lime and palm sugar 92
    nuôc mám 98
    sabayon 133
    tamarind dipping 96
    Thai mint dressing 106
    yoghurt chilli 88
Selva Rajah, Carol 22, 67, 94–5, *94*, 118–121, *119*, *120*

cooking with beer 70, 71 85
combining with beer 65, 68, 69, 73
shellfish recipes
    chicken and squid salad 98, *99*
    chili ketam (chilli crab) 94, *94*
    chillli and black bean mud crab braised with ale 113
    jhinga kari (south Indian prawn curry) *110*, 111
    mussels cooked in white beer 83
    oyster beignets with gribiche sauce 86, *87*
    prawns cooked in beer 112
    prawns sautéed with beer and lime 93
    salad of cuttlefish, pawpaw chilli, lime and cashews *2*, *22*, 92
    seafood and lemongrass broth *109*, 112
soup
    cooking with beer 73, 85
soup and broth recipes
    fast beer 22, 79
    German beer 85
    mussels cooked in white beer 83
    onion with lager 82, *82*
    seafood and lemongrass *109*, 112
Sparrow, Kate 98, *99*
spice 18, 67, 73, 84, 118–120
spice mix 105
spiced peaches 108
Squire, James 14, 60
stout 41, 67, 85, 135
    sorbet 85, *85*, 136, *137*

strong ale 37, 40
Sumeria 49, 64
sushi 64, 66, 69, 73

tart, dark valhrona chocolate *132*, 133
tavern talk 123, 131
Taylor, Chris 96
tea, popularity of 17–18
terrine
    smoked salmon 90, *91*
    veal and bacon 117
Thirkell, Angela 16
Thomas, Richard 69, 134–5
Tomlin, Liam 90, *91*, 117
Trappist ale 37, 39, 47
truffle burger 107, *107*

vanilla ice cream with chocolate stout sauce and malt praline *129*, 130
vintage beer 38, 46

Welsh rabbit 78
weisse-stye wheat beer 42
weizen wheat beer 42
wheat beer, varieties and brand names 41–2
wine, beer matches 73, 100–101

yeast 13, 27, 52-3

zucchini
    braised 97
    flowers battered with goat's cheese 79